I0752572

On the Trail of Billy the Kid

A Photographic Journey of His Life and Death in New Mexico

On the Trail of Billy the Kid

A Photographic Journey of His Life and Death in New Mexico

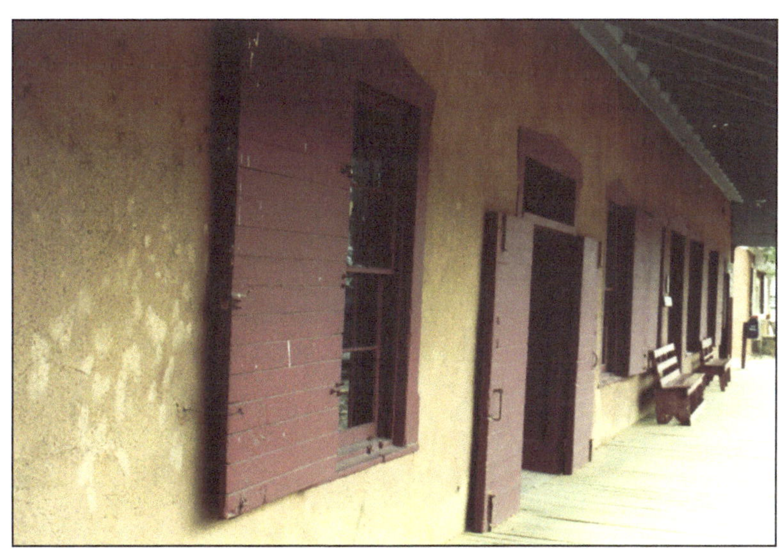

Lori Ann Goodloe

Revised and Expanded
Second Edition

Previously published in limited edition in 2009.

Goodloe, Lori Ann
On the Trail of Billy the Kid: A Photographic Journey of His Life and Death in New Mexico
ISBN: 979-8-9913188-9-1 (paperback ed.)

Book design by Lori Ann Goodloe
Front and Back Covers: Billy's Grave, Fort Sumner, July 14, 2012

Printed and bound in the United States of America

For Billy

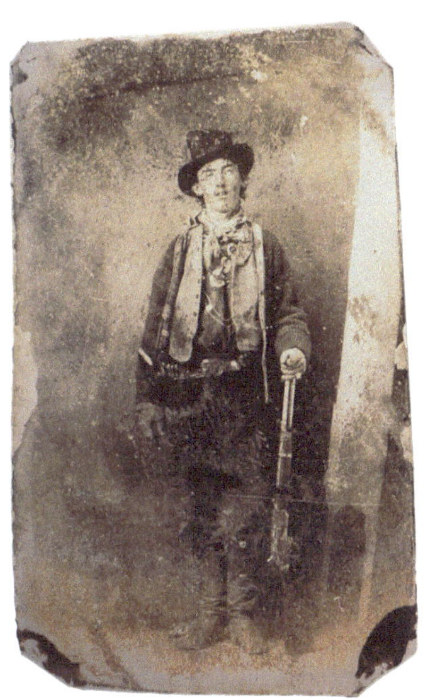

Preface

When I started this journey, I was naïve enough to think that history would be preserved. It has been over 140 years since Pat Garrett killed Billy the Kid and nothing remains the same. His mother's laundry business in Wichita is a parking lot; a visitors' center and a movie prop have replaced the house in Silver City where he grew up; and the courthouse where he was tried is now a gift shop. Even Billy's grave is caged, and his footstone is shackled to the ground to deter theft. By carefully avoiding the inconvenient telephone pole, gas station, or *no trespassing* sign, I did my best to maintain the historical integrity of Billy's New Mexico.

I grew up hearing the stories of Billy the Kid, and through my research, he has become more than just a legend in a book. As I walked where he walked and saw what he saw, he became a real person. These photographs represent his short life in the Territory of New Mexico, the territory he loved and could not bear to leave, even with a price on his head.

Opposite Page Top: Ron Howard donated this replica of an 1870s cabin from his movie, *The Missing,* as a stand-in for Billy's childhood home in Silver City.

Opposite Page Bottom: Billy's caged grave in Fort Sumner

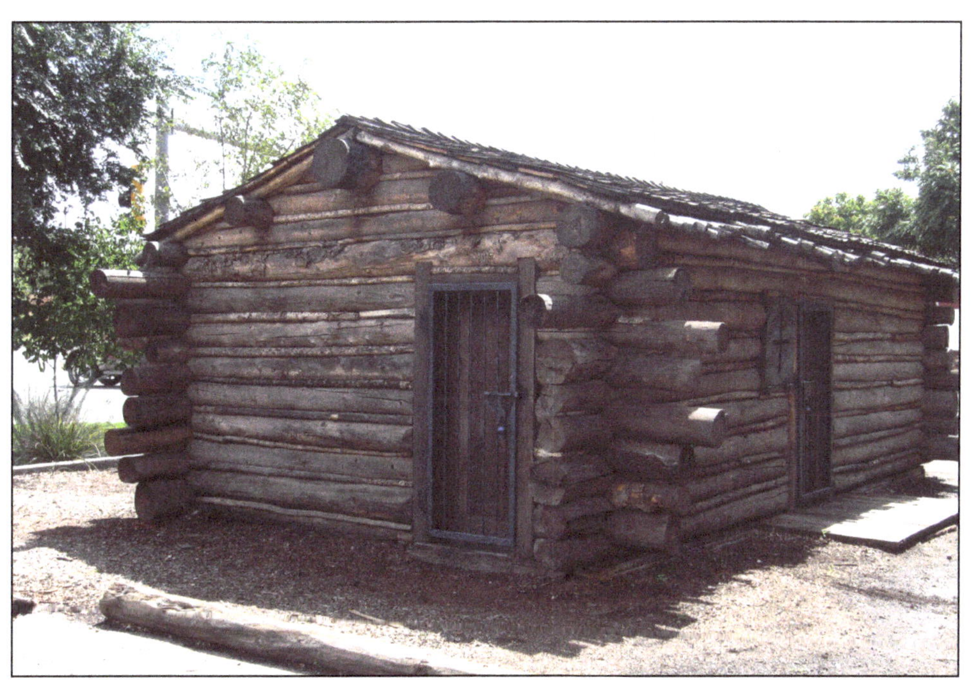

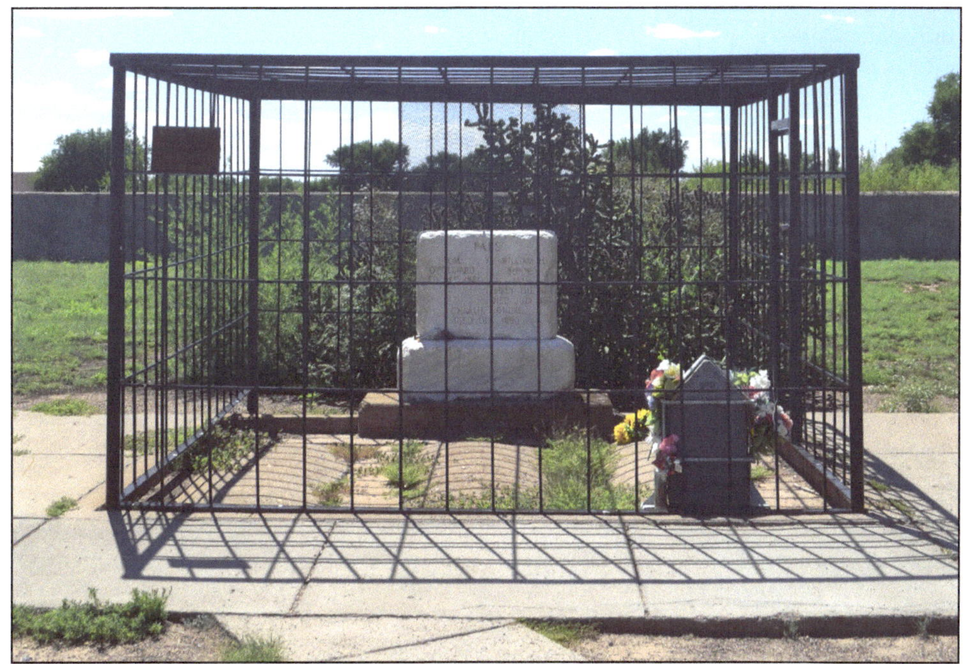

Santa Fe

The birthplace of Billy the Kid is a mystery. Historians are still trying to discover any verified documentation of where the Kid was born. The most popular contender is New York, but Ireland, Indiana, and Missouri are all in the running. We also don't know when he was born. Ash Upson, the ghostwriter for Pat Garrett's book, *The Authentic Life of Billy the Kid*, who also claimed to know Billy as a child, said Billy's birthdate was November 23, 1859. This date is suspicious because November 23 is also Upson's birthday, which is how he claimed to remember it. Recent research shows Billy's birth year may have been closer to 1862, but like his birthplace, nothing has been definitively proven.

Regardless of where or when he was born, we know his name was William Henry McCarty. We also know he had a mother named Catherine and a brother named Joseph; the identity of his father, however, is yet another mystery.

The beginning of Billy's documented history begins in Anderson, Indiana, in June of 1868, when his family was recorded in the local census. The trail picks up again in Wichita, Kansas, in 1870, where Catherine owned land, ran a laundry, and was the only woman to sign the petition for the town's incorporation. The family was only there for about a year before moving on. Catherine suffered from tuberculosis, and she moved further and further west, seeking a better climate for her condition. The family possibly moved to Denver, Colorado after Wichita, but the next recorded evidence shows Catherine and her sons in Santa Fe, New Mexico.

On March 1, 1873, at the First Presbyterian Church of Santa Fe, Catherine married William Antrim, whom she had met several years prior. Billy and Joseph signed the register as witnesses. William Antrim adopted the two boys, and Billy started going by the name Henry Antrim—probably to avoid any confusion between him and his stepfather.

The family didn't stay long in Santa Fe, and shortly after the wedding, the Antrims moved again—this time to Silver City.

Opposite Page: Founded in 1867, the First Presbyterian Church is the oldest Protestant church in New Mexico. The original adobe structure was replaced with red brick in 1881, and in the 143 years since, it has sustained damage from a fire and undergone several renovations.

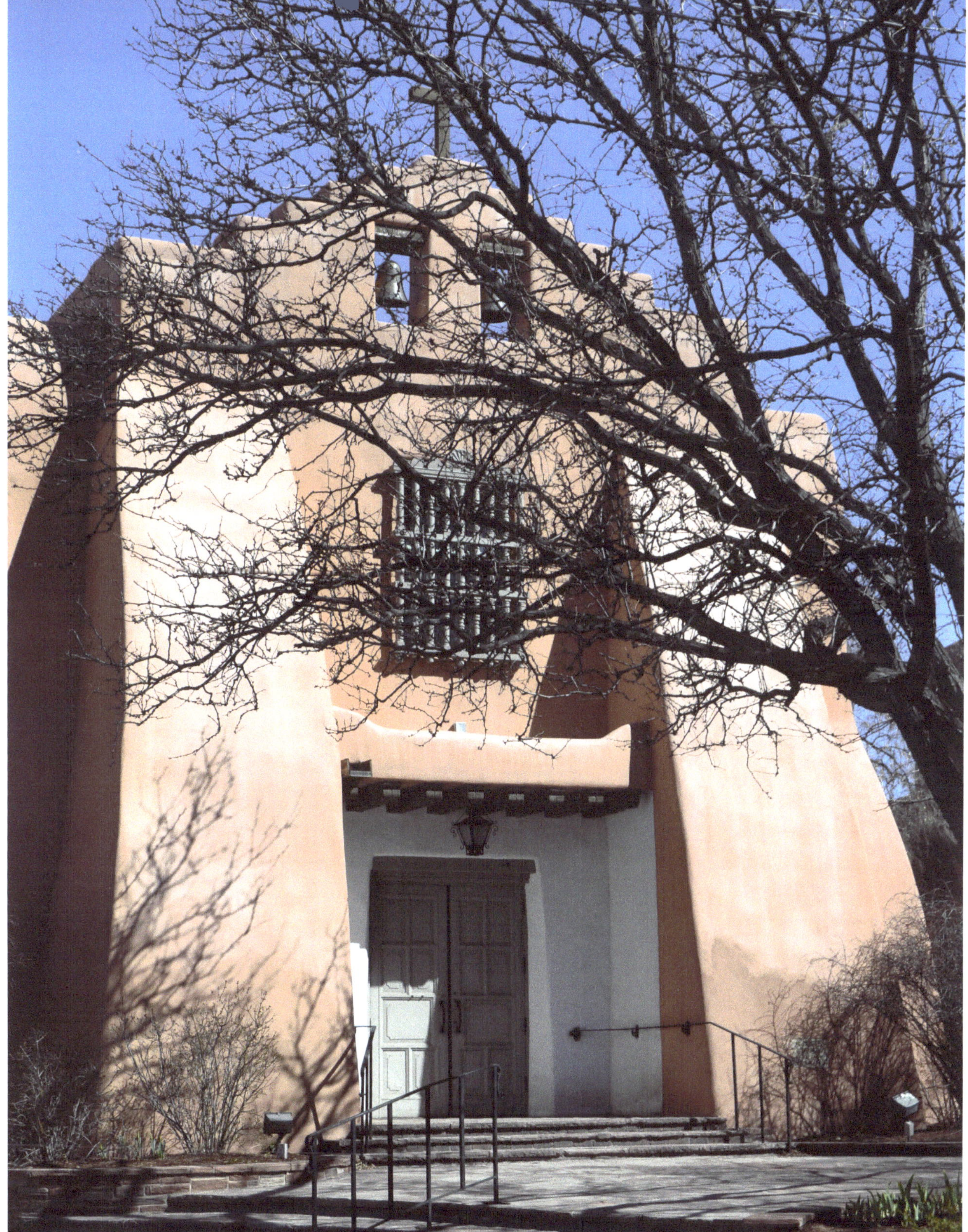

Silver City

Those who grew up with Henry in Silver City said he was no more of a troublemaker than any other boy his age. He enjoyed school and got along well with his teacher. He liked performing in plays and attending dances with his mother. For the most part, his early days in Silver City were perfectly normal, and, in their recollections, the ones who knew him best remembered him fondly.

But things quickly changed when his mother's health grew worse, and she became bedridden. William Antrim spent most of his time away from home, meaning Henry and Joseph likely took on the responsibility of caring for their dying mother. Sadly, Catherine succumbed to tuberculosis on September 16, 1874, when Henry was still a boy. Had she lived, his life probably would have turned out much differently.

After his wife's death, Antrim completely abandoned his stepsons, sending them to live with different families in town. Henry went to live with the Truesdell family and worked in their hotel, washing dishes and doing odd chores—Mrs. Truesdell once commented that Henry was the only boy who didn't steal the silverware. However, he didn't live long with the Truesdell family before being uprooted again, this time moving in with a family named Brown. While at the Brown home, Henry became enamored with another lodger and a local thief nicknamed Sombrero Jack. In September of 1875, Sombrero Jack broke into a Chinese laundry and stole clothes, blankets, and guns, giving the shirts to Henry to hide. Mrs. Brown found the stolen shirts and informed Sheriff Harvey Whitehill, who then arrested Henry even though he knew the boy hadn't committed the crime.

Henry had had his fair share of scrapes with the law when his mother was sick and he was fending for himself. But this time, the crime was more serious, and Whitehill wanted to teach the boy a lesson to scare him straight. Henry, however, thought he was in much more trouble than he was and devised an escape plan. After only one day in jail, Henry talked Whitehill into letting him walk the hallway outside his cell for exercise. Whitehill obliged and released Henry from the cell but locked him in the building while he left for the morning. Once alone, Henry crawled into the large fireplace and climbed up the chimney, making the first of many jailbreaks in his short career.

Believing himself a wanted fugitive, Henry sought help from a family friend, who put him on a stagecoach bound for Arizona.

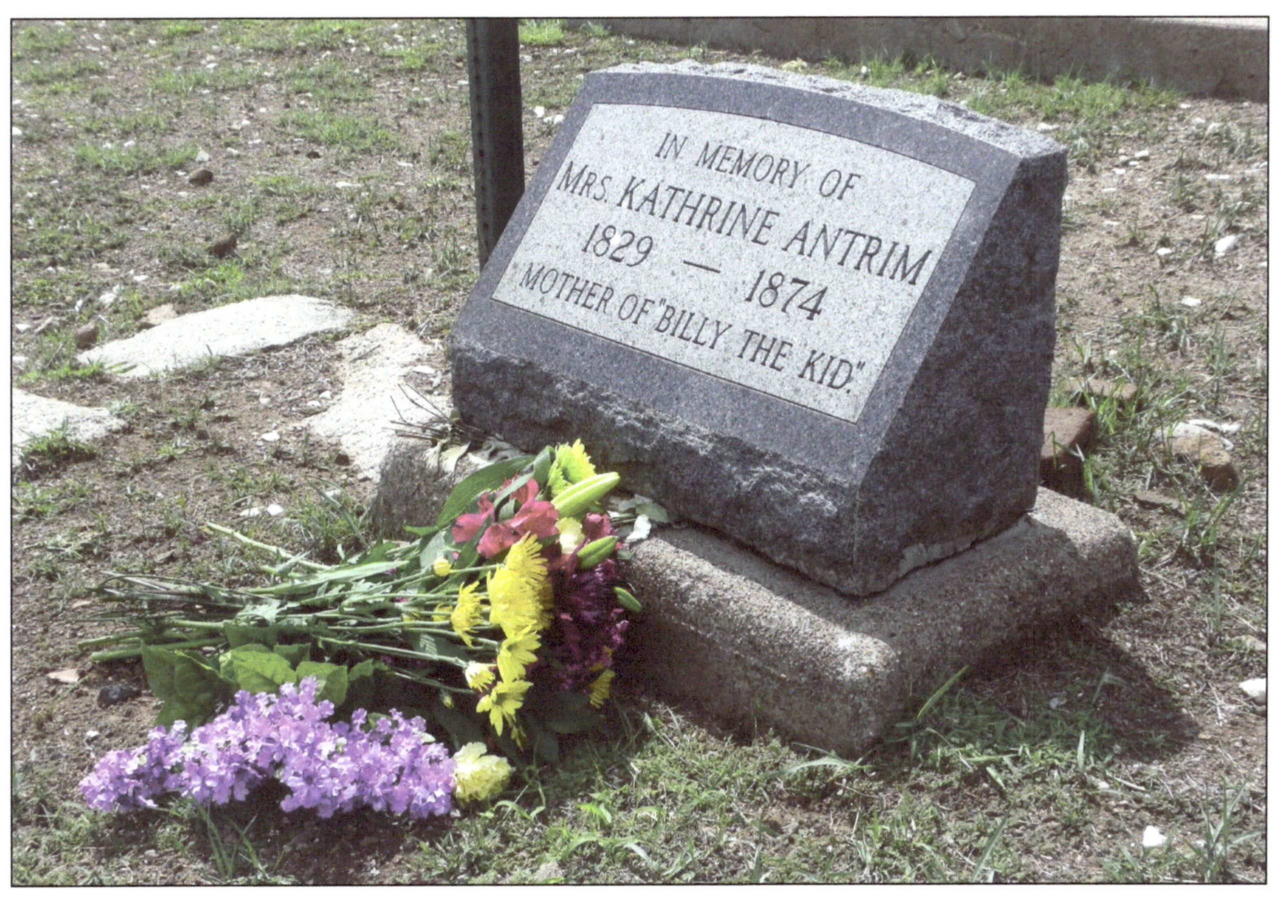

The mother of "Billy the Kid" can be found in Memory Lane Cemetery in Silver City. Unfortunately, Catherine's name was misspelled when her wooden marker was replaced with the current headstone.

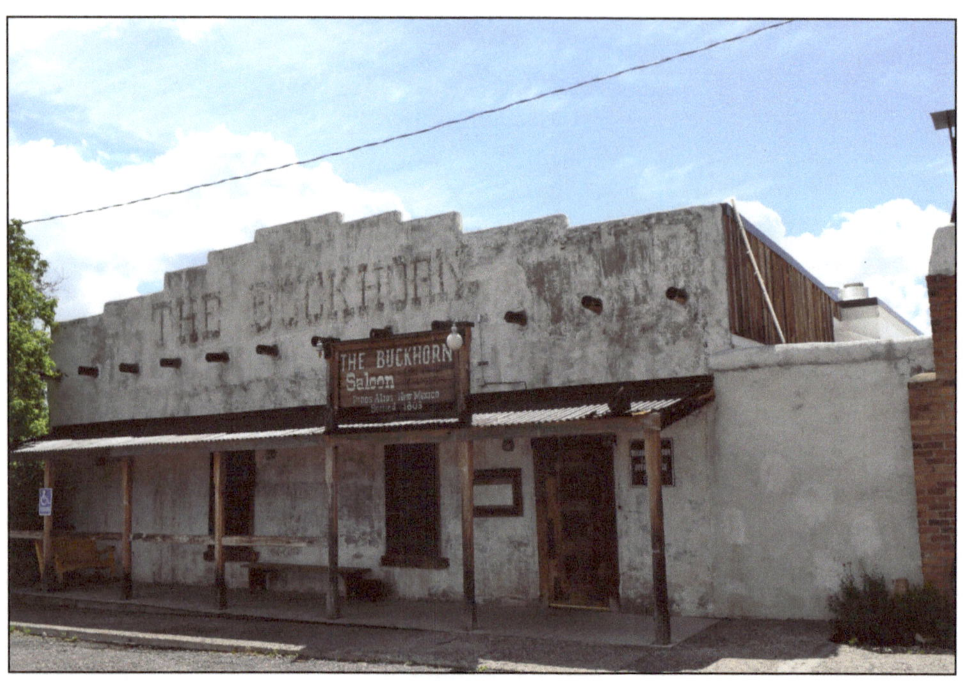

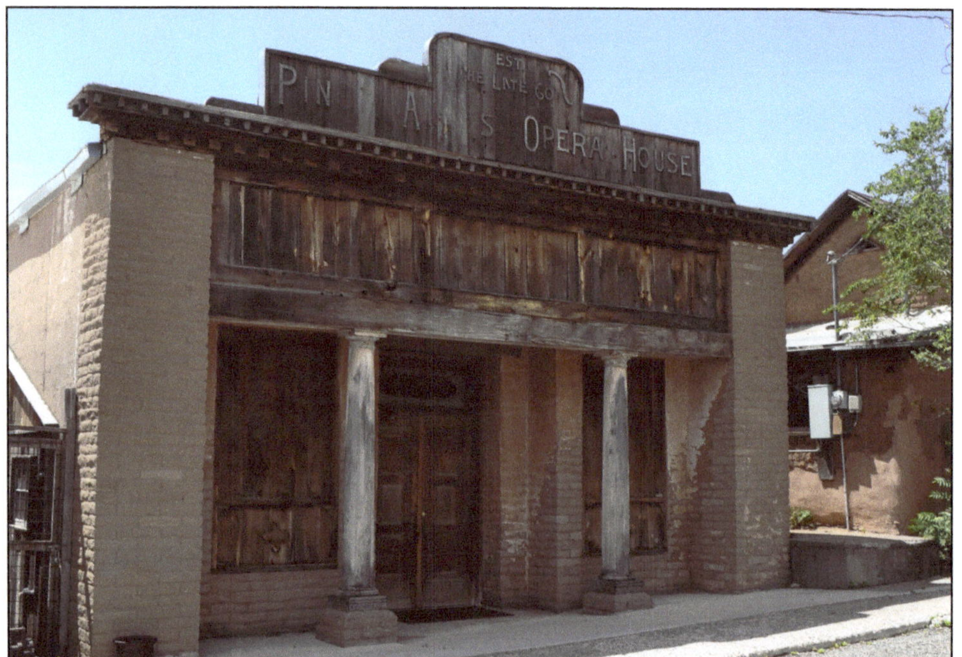

Piños Altos was a small mining town six miles north of Silver City. The Buckhorn Saloon (top) and the Opera House (bottom) opened in the 1860s, and it's thought that Henry would have attended dances here with his mother before her health declined.

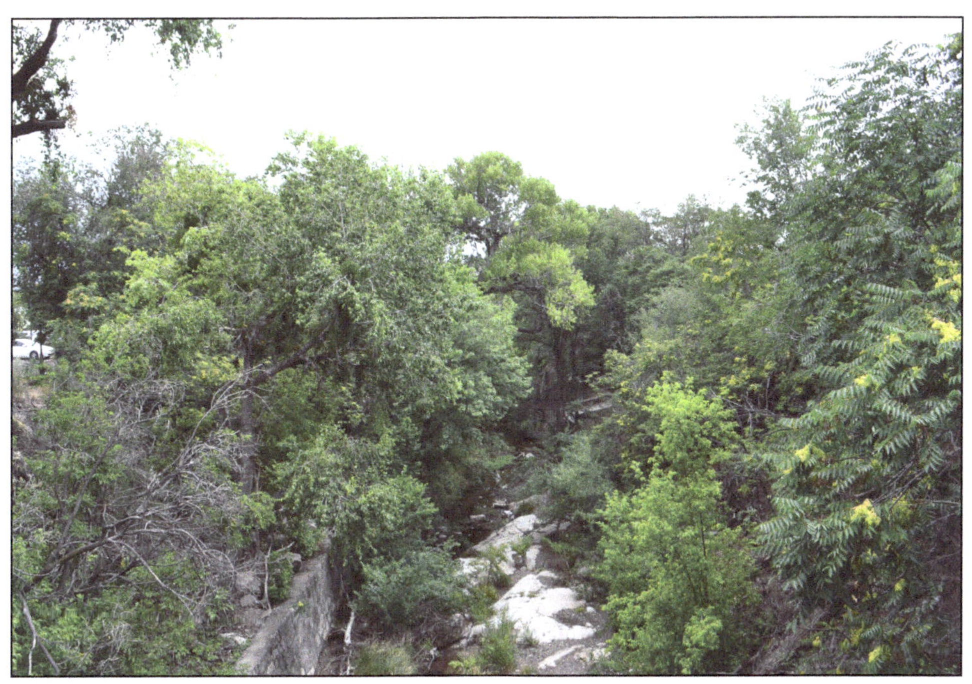

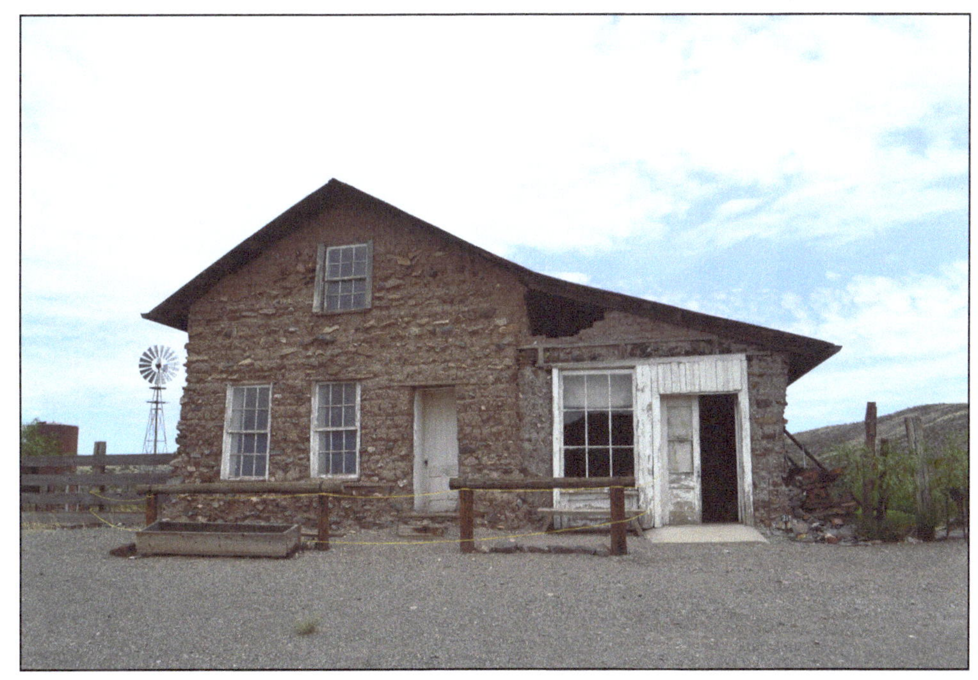

Top: Due to massive floods in 1895 and 1902, Main Street, where the Antrims lived in Silver City, was washed away and has since been replaced by what the locals call the "Big Ditch."

Bottom: The Stratford Hotel in Shakespeare, New Mexico, where, after running from Silver City, Henry was said to have washed dishes for a short time before moving on to Arizona.

Arizona

By the fall of 1875, and for two years after, Henry found himself in eastern Arizona, bouncing around between Fort Grant, Globe, and the San Carlos Indian Reservation. Now going by the name Kid Antrim, he did his best to make a living by gambling and stealing horses but wasn't very successful. Henry was arrested more than once and managed to escape each time.

In August 1877, Henry was back in Fort Grant, and it was here he killed his first man: Frank "Windy" Cahill. A blacksmith and a bully, Cahill targeted Henry the moment he first arrived in town, physically abusing and humiliating the boy every chance he got. It's even believed that Cahill fitted Henry for shackles during one of his arrests, something Cahill would have greatly enjoyed. It's safe to say Henry hated Cahill.

On the night of August 17, 1877, Henry and Cahill were playing cards in Atkin's Saloon and argued. Cahill called Henry a pimp, and Henry called Cahill a son-of-a-bitch—a moment later, Cahill grabbed Henry, threw him to the ground, and started hitting him. Henry, being much younger and smaller than Cahill, was outmatched and likely would have been beaten to death if he hadn't been armed. Henry was able to reach a pistol he had concealed in his trousers and shot Cahill in the stomach. Cahill collapsed, and Henry fled before Cahill's friends could catch him. He stole the fastest horse outside and rode back to New Mexico.

Opposite Page Top: The site of Atkin's Saloon in present-day Bonita, Arizona

Opposite Page Bottom: Windy Cahill, the Kid's first victim is buried in the Bonita Cemetery.

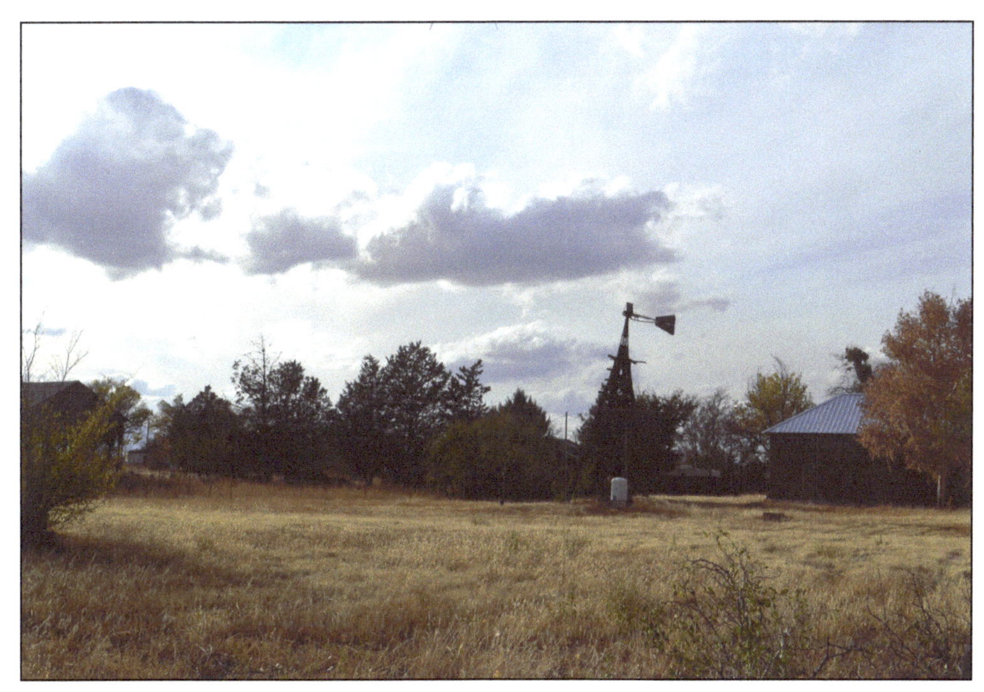

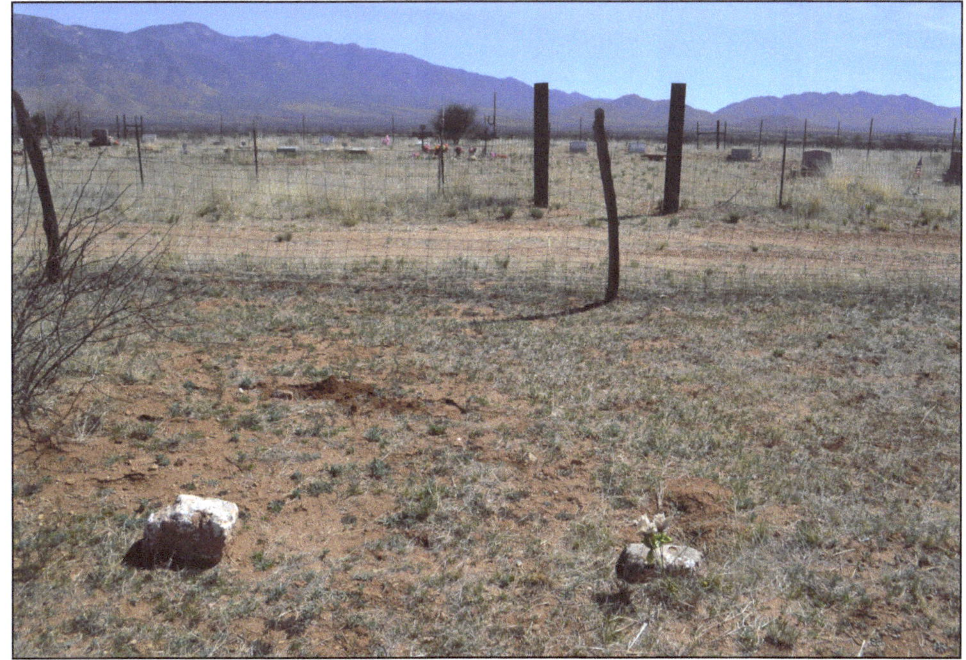

Doña Ana County

After running from Fort Grant, the Kid wound up back in southern New Mexico, this time making a home for himself in Doña Ana County. Here, he joined a notorious group of rustlers and murderers known as "the Boys," led by a young man named Jesse Evans.

Now going by his most well-known alias of William H. Bonney (or Billy), the Kid spent a short time with Evans' gang, stealing horses and cattle from ranchers all over southern New Mexico. One rancher who was a particular target of Evans' gang was John Chisum, the most prominent cattle baron in those parts. Chisum had claimed all the middle-river country as his own, effectively controlling the best land in New Mexico. Chisum competed directly with L. G. Murphy & Co. for the Army and Indian reservation beef contracts. Murphy and his partner James Dolan, neither known for their honesty, frequently bought Chisum's stolen cattle from Evans.

Billy only spent a short time rustling with Evans before the two had a falling out. Billy left the gang and made his way up north to Lincoln County, where he met the man who would forever change his life: John Tunstall.

Opposite Page: Picacho Peak overlooks Mesilla, Las Cruces, and Doña Ana.

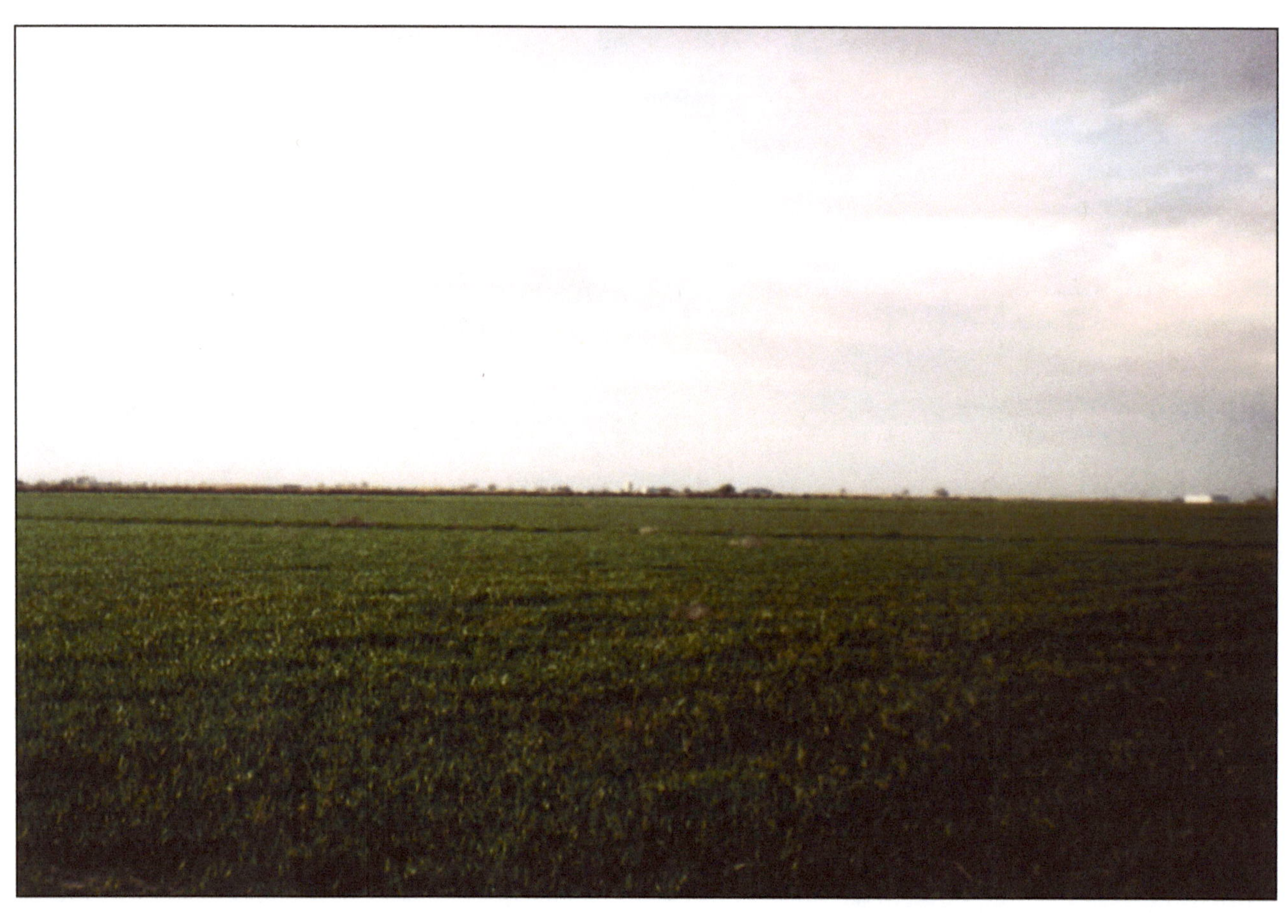

John Chisum's land spread out over present-day Artesia...

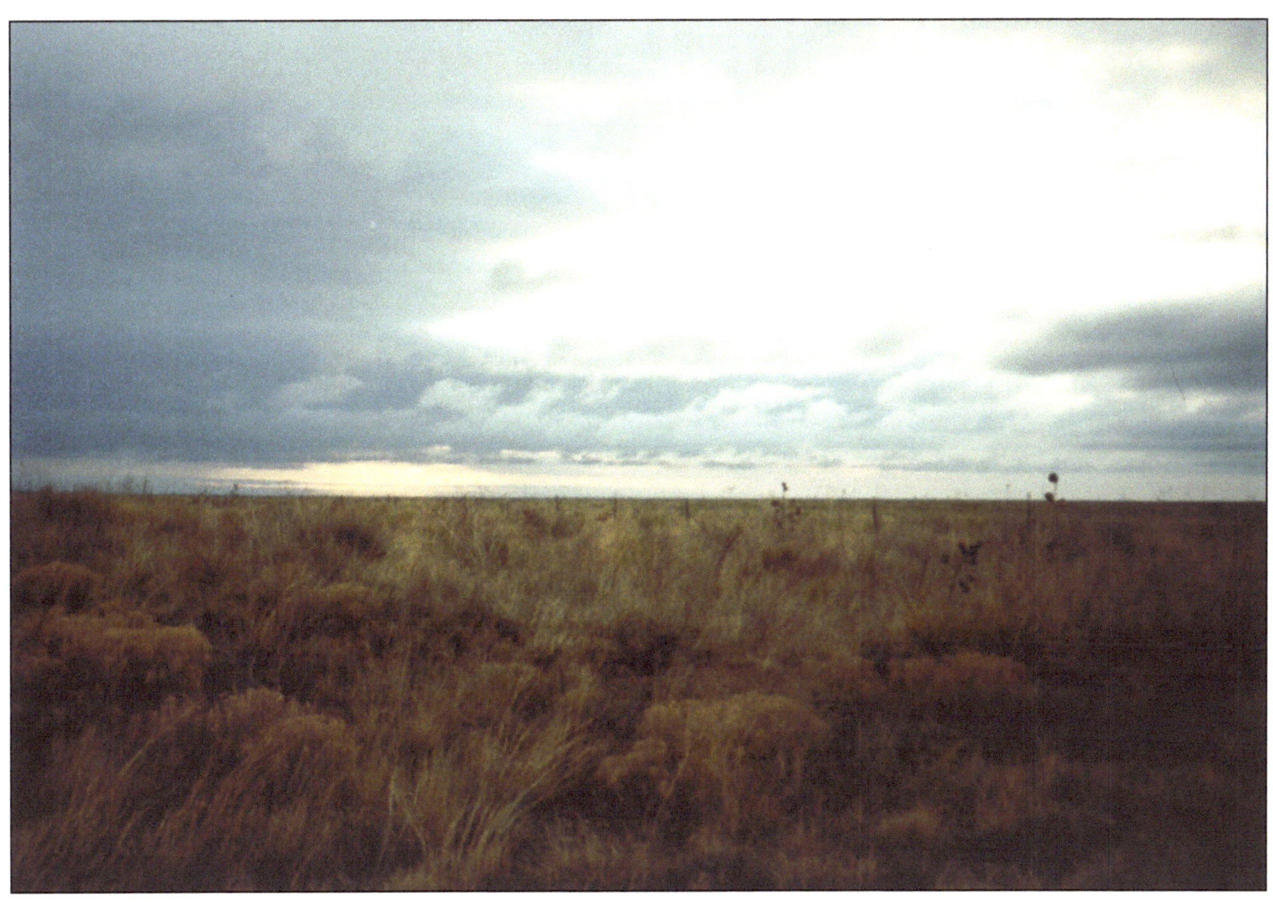

...and Roswell.

John H. Tunstall

Born in London, England, John Henry Tunstall was working for his father's mercantile company in British Columbia when he decided he would rather be a rancher in America. After convincing his father that it would be a good investment, the twenty-three-year-old left Canada for California to try his hand at sheep ranching. However, since cheap land was scarce in California, Tunstall settled in New Mexico instead.

He first went to Santa Fe, where he met several prominent men from Lincoln, including a lawyer named Alexander McSween. McSween convinced Tunstall that there was land and opportunity to be had in Lincoln County. He also told the young Englishman of Murphy and Dolan's dominance of not only the beef contracts but of Lincoln County itself. L. G. Murphy & Co., known locally as "the House," had control of most economic resources in the area: land, mercantile, and cattle. McSween convinced Tunstall that he should go up against the House, and with McSween's legal help and knowledge of House business, they could end Murphy and Dolan's stranglehold on Lincoln.

Excited by this prospect, Tunstall moved to Lincoln in November 1876. He bought cattle and horses and started a ranch south of Lincoln on the Rio Feliz. He also opened a mercantile store in town, just down the street from the House.

It was during this time that Billy first met Tunstall after he was caught stealing Tunstall's horses. Rather than prosecute the boy, Tunstall hired him, giving him a horse, a saddle, and a Winchester rifle. Billy was heard to say that Tunstall was the only one, other than his mother, who had ever treated him right, earning him the Kid's unwavering loyalty.

Opposite Page: The Tunstall store in Lincoln exterior (top) and interior (bottom)

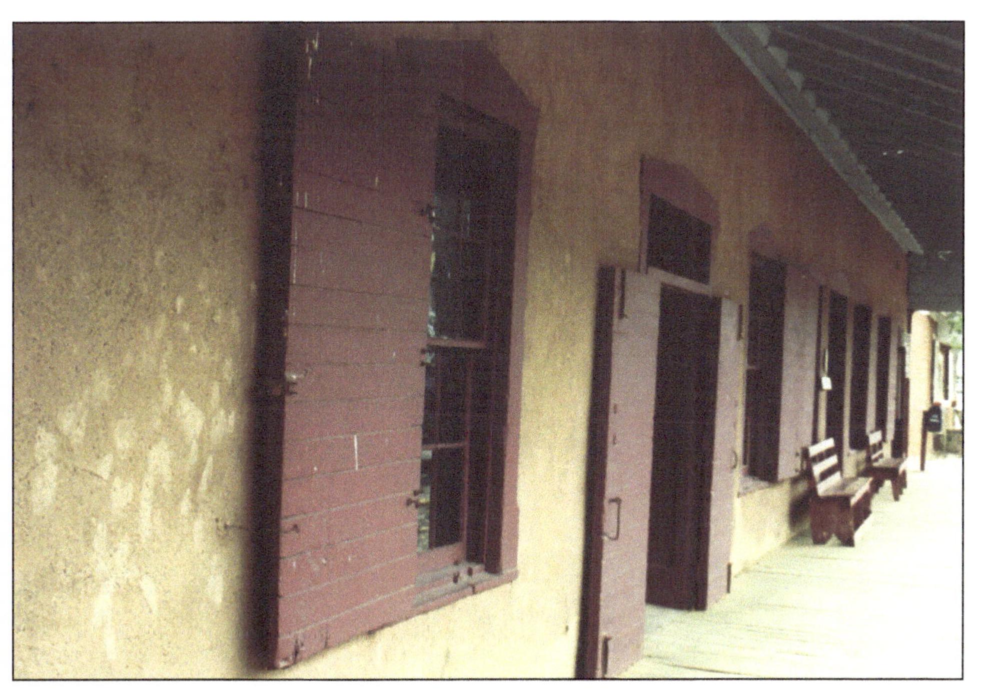

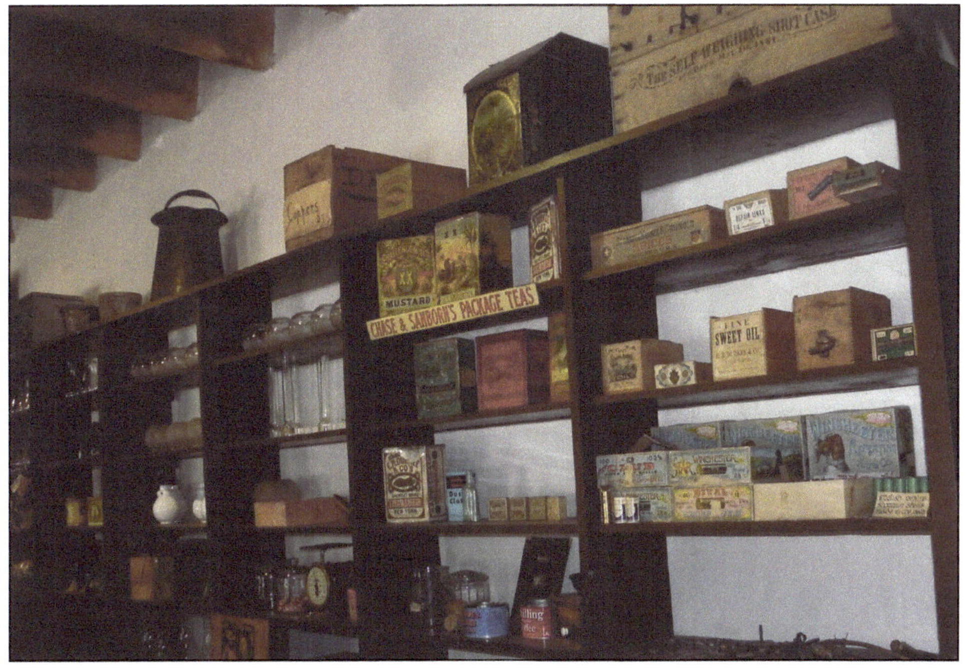
MUSTARD
CHASE & SANBORN'S PACKAGE TEAS
FINE
SWEET OIL

The Lincoln County War
Part I

When Tunstall set up the J. H. Tunstall store down the street from the House, he was by no means welcome. Greed was the main reason for the Lincoln County War—a desire for money, land, and power. However, the hatred stemming from both factions intertwined throughout the short history of the county. Because Murphy had been increasing his cattle supply by buying John Chisum's stolen cattle from Jesse Evans and his gang, Chisum also figured prominently in the story. Chisum may not have technically been a partner of Tunstall and McSween, but he certainly supported their side. Billy found his way into the tangled saga by parting ways with Evans and joining Tunstall, making himself an enemy of Murphy twice over.

By January 1877, feuding between the two factions escalated when Dolan used his political connections in Santa Fe to make life miserable for Tunstall and McSween. McSween had unrelated legal problems, and as a result, most of his assets were seized. Sheriff Brady, a Murphy-Dolan cohort, not only took McSween's property but Tunstall's as well, erroneously claiming it was because the two men were partners. This illegal act sent Tunstall to seek justice from the law rather than a weapon (the typical problem-solver in the territory). But Tunstall never had the chance to realize that trying to find justice in the crooked systems of New Mexico was futile.

On February 18, 1878, Tunstall and his men, including Billy, Dick Brewer, John Middleton, and Rob Widenmann, were en route to Lincoln from Tunstall's ranch with a herd of horses not yet seized by Brady. They hadn't traveled far from the ranch before spotting a flock of wild turkeys. While his men rode off in pursuit of the birds, Tunstall stayed with the horses. From a distance, they heard a posse of about twenty-five men, hired by Dolan and Brady and led by Bill Morton, ride up behind Tunstall. Middleton tried to warn Tunstall as he and the others took cover, but Tunstall seemed confused and failed to get away. By then, it was too late; Tunstall's men were too far away and in no position to help as their boss was murdered.

It's believed that Morton shot Tunstall in the chest while Frank Baker killed Tunstall's horse, and either Jesse Evans or Tom Hill (accounts vary) shot the already-dead man in the back of the head. Sheriff Whitehill once said that if "someone did [Billy] dirt then he would seek revenge." The murder of his boss certainly qualified; Billy vowed vengeance.

When Tunstall's men returned to Lincoln with the news of the murder, Constable Antonio Martinez took Billy and another of Tunstall's men, Fred Waite, to arrest the men responsible. Sheriff Brady, however, refused to arrest the guilty men and instead arrested Billy, Martinez, and Waite for disturbing the peace and confiscated the rifle Tunstall had given to Billy. Martinez was released later that day, but Brady only released Billy and Waite after they missed Tunstall's funeral.

On learning of his friend's death, McSween, a devoutly religious man, also opted to turn to the law. Brewer, who had been Tunstall's foreman, was made a deputy constable and assembled a posse of eleven other deputized men who became known as the Regulators. These men had the authority to arrest the men who participated in Tunstall's murder.

In March, the Regulators captured and arrested Morton and Baker. However, the prisoners never made it back to Lincoln alive. According to the Regulators, both men were killed while trying to escape. Even though Morton and Baker were undoubtedly involved in Tunstall's murder, their suspicious deaths hurt the Regulators' cause. But it didn't compare to what came next.

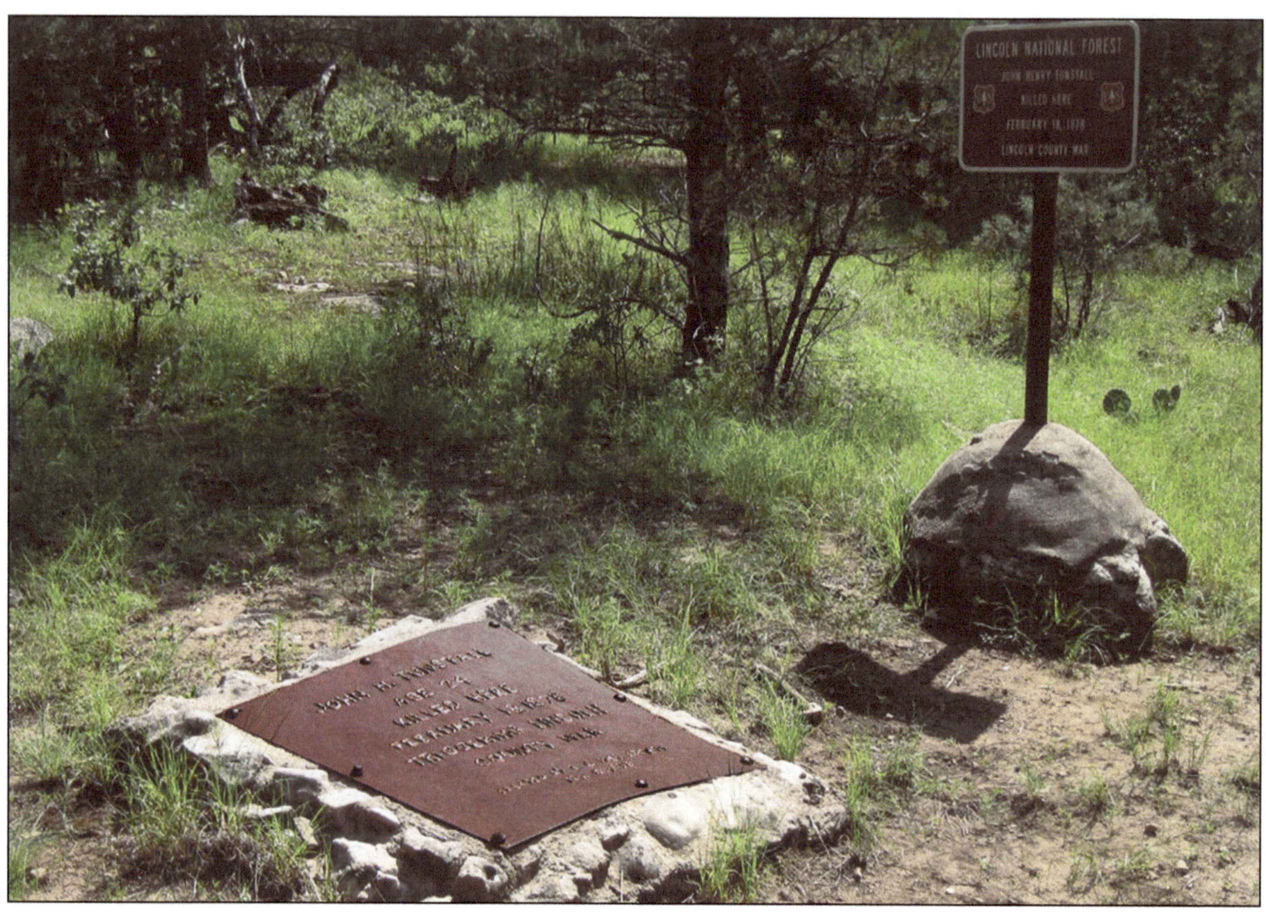

Above: The site of Tunstall's murder in what's now known as Tunstall Canyon in Glencoe

Opposite Page: Tunstall's grave marker behind his store in Lincoln

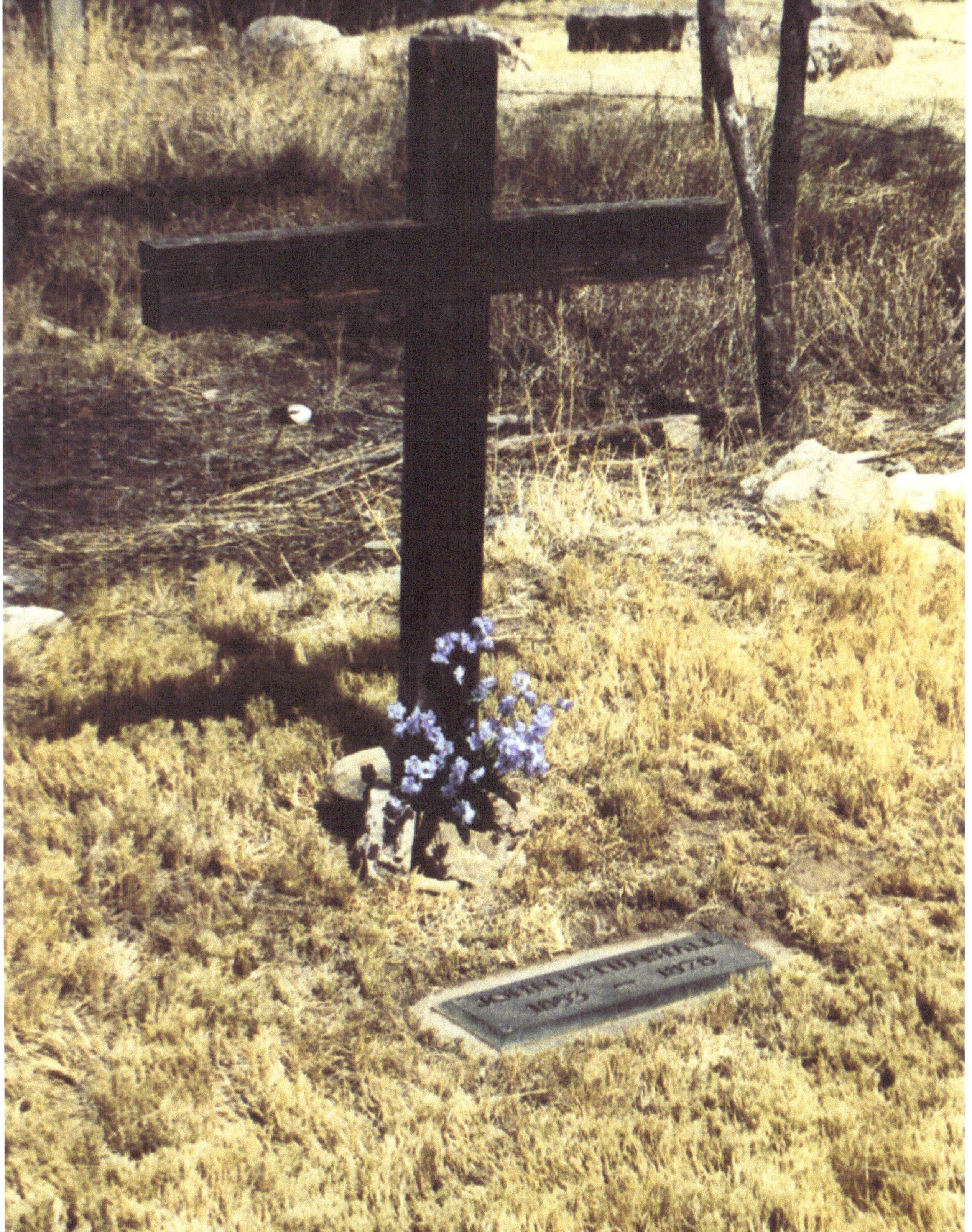

Sheriff Brady

On the morning of April 1, 1878, several Regulators, including Billy, were in the Tunstall store gathering supplies when they spotted Sheriff Brady approaching. Brady, along with his deputies, Billy Mathews, George Hindman, George Peppin, and Jack Long, were walking down the street from the House to the courthouse. When they spotted Brady, the Regulators did one of the most reckless things they could have done and made the rash decision to ambush and kill the sheriff.

From behind an adobe wall in front of Tunstall's corral, Billy and five others, John Middleton, Fred Waite, Henry Brown, Jim French, and Frank MacNab, fired on Brady and his deputies. Brady and Hindman both fell, and the others scattered for cover. Billy and French ran into the street to retrieve the Winchester Brady had confiscated from Billy after Tunstall's murder. From his hiding place, Mathews fired on Billy and French, winging them both and forcing them to retreat into the Tunstall store. Moments later, the Regulators tore out of the corral and rode out of town.

Even though Billy and the others felt justified in their actions, the townsfolk weren't as forgiving. Brady may have been a crooked lawman, but he was still a lawman. He died riddled with bullet holes, and the lawless act further sullied the reputation of the Regulators. And even though Billy claimed later that he was shooting at Mathews, the murder of Sheriff Brady would come back to haunt him.

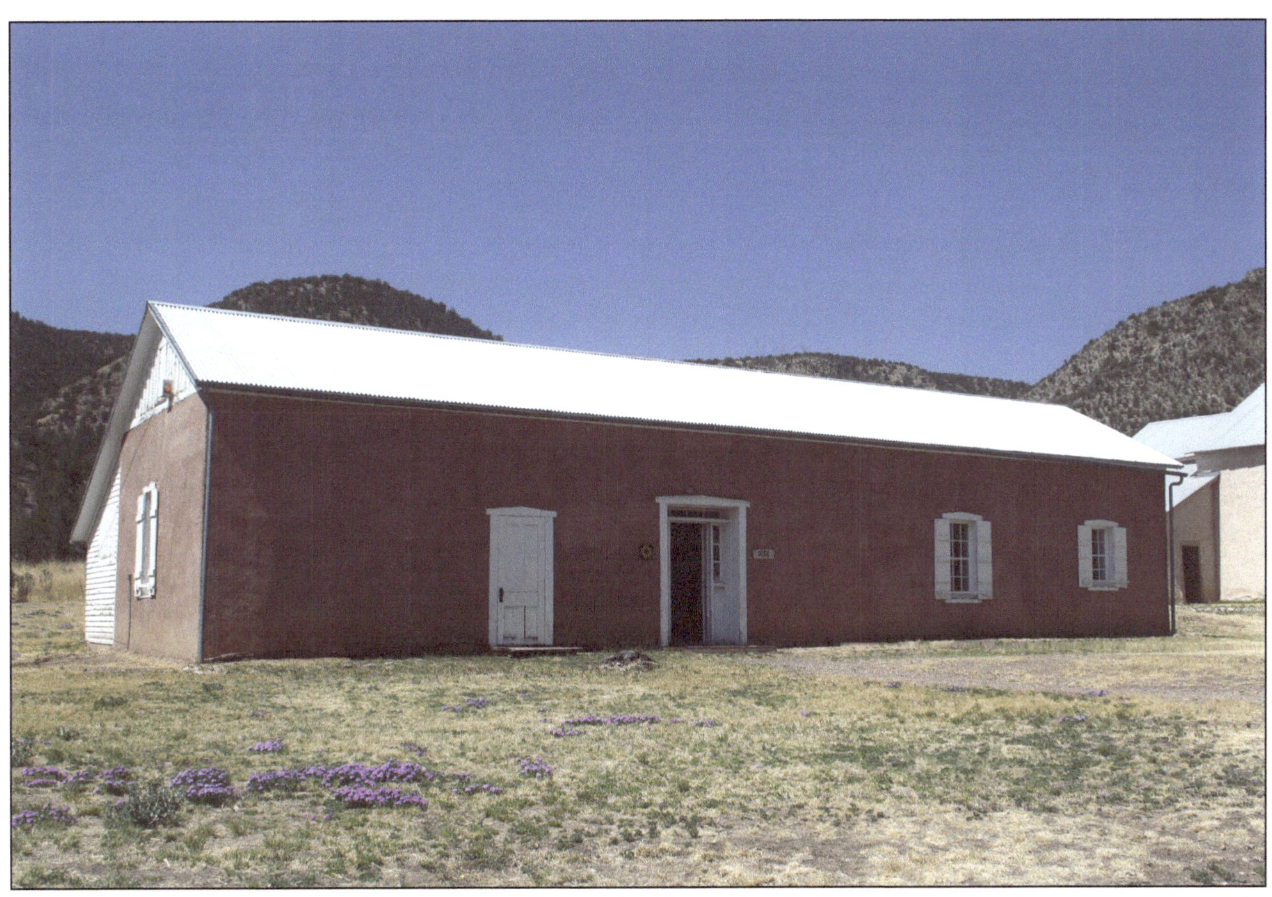

The original courthouse in Lincoln, where Brady was headed when he was ambushed

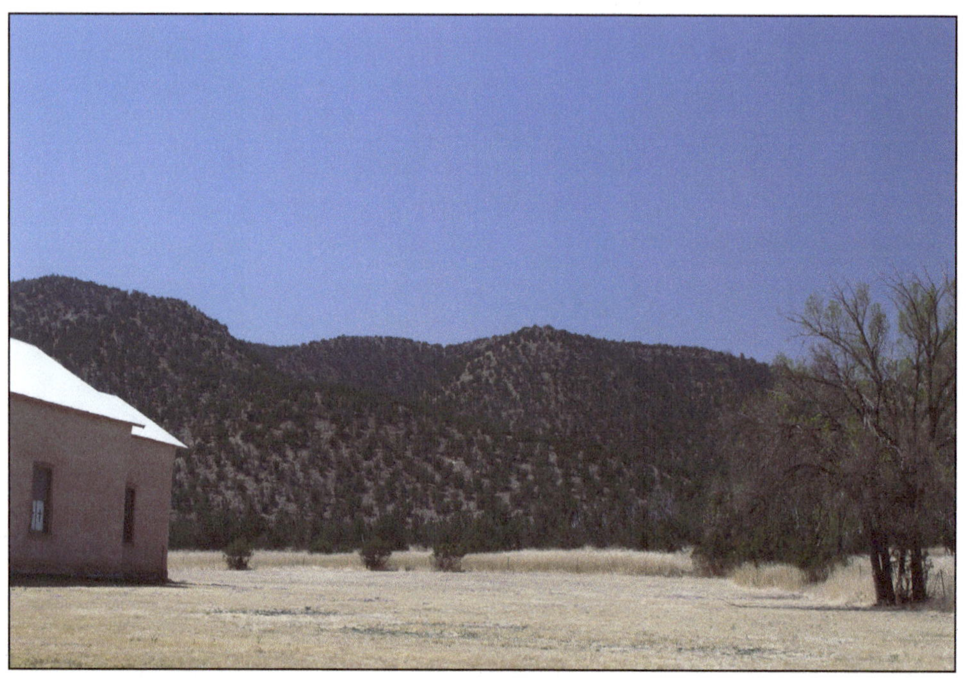

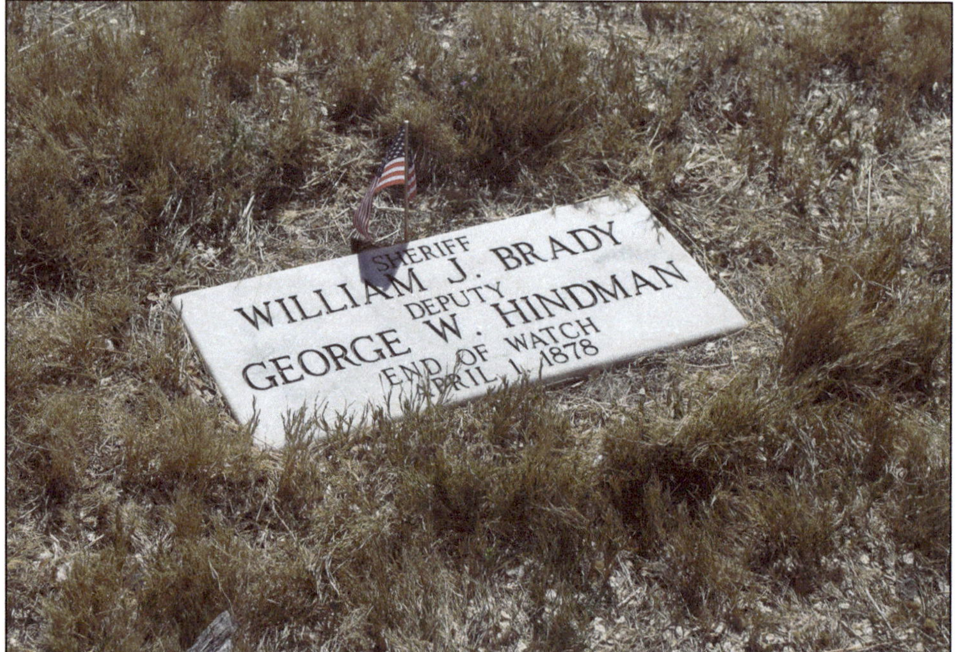

Top: The site of Squire Wilson's home. Wilson was tending his onion patch during the shootout and was hit in the thigh with an errant bullet.

Bottom: The site of Brady and Hindman's murder

Opposite Page: It's believed that after Mathews hit the Kid and Jim French, one of them (stories differ on who) ran to safety in the back room of the Tunstall store and hid under the floorboards while soldiers from Fort Stanton searched for them above.

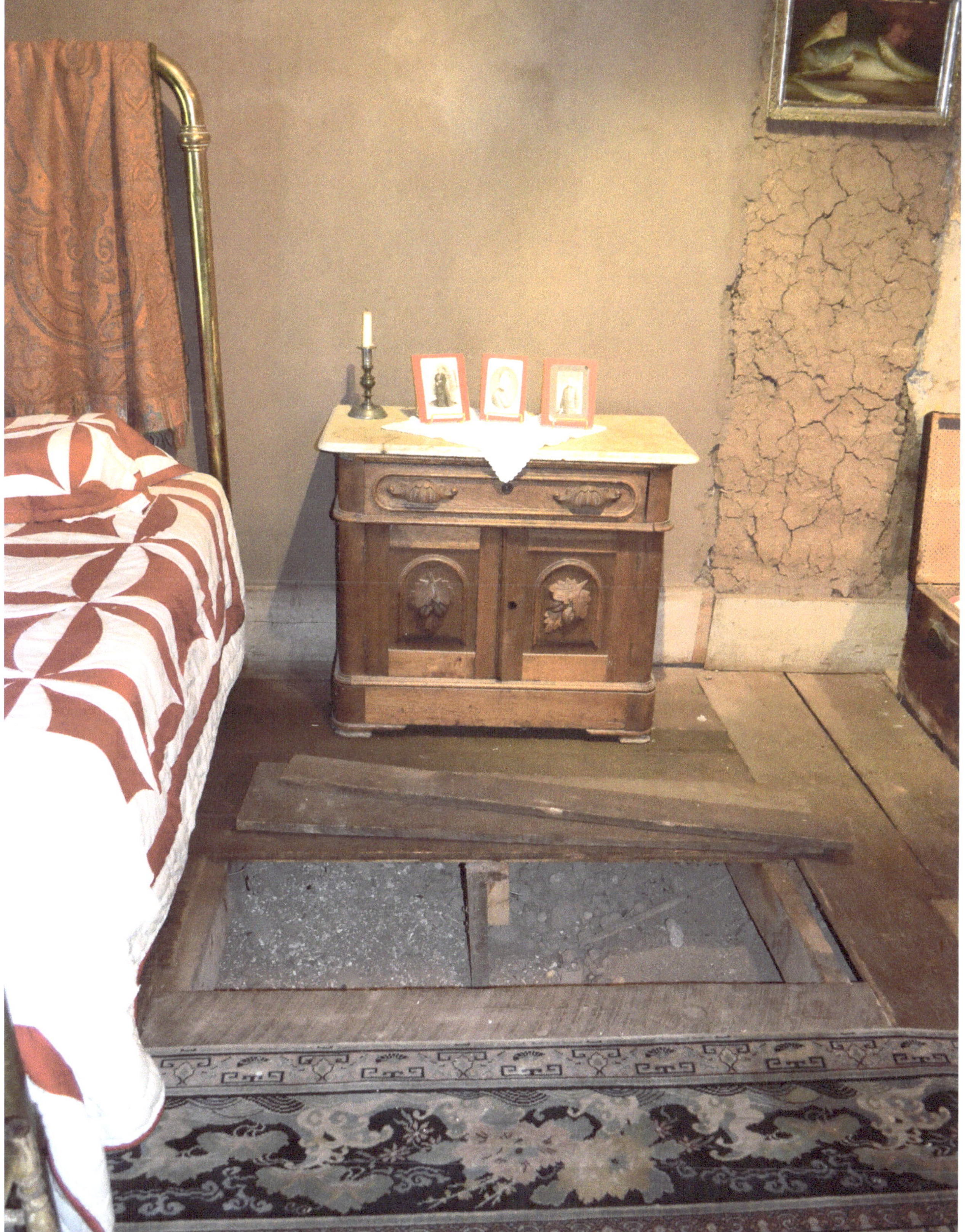

Blazer's Mill

A few days after Brady's murder, the Regulators rode onto the Mescalero Apache Indian Reservation, still searching for Tunstall's killers. As they passed through, they stopped to eat at Blazer's Mill, where soon after, "Buckshot" Roberts also rode in. They had a warrant for Roberts' arrest, and because Frank Coe knew Roberts, he went outside and tried to convince him to surrender peacefully. Roberts refused. Meanwhile, Charlie Bowdre, George Coe, Frank MacNab, and Henry Brown came out to corner Roberts. Bowdre demanded that Roberts surrender. When Roberts again refused, both men drew their weapons and fired. Bowdre's shot hit Roberts in the stomach, while Roberts' shot hit Bowdre's cartridge belt before ricocheting and severing off George Coe's trigger finger.

The others quickly entered the fight, but Roberts proved more dangerous than all the Regulators combined. After hitting Bowdre and Coe, Roberts' next shot hit Middleton in the chest; another shot wounded Doc Scurlock, and yet another shot grazed Billy as he entered the fray.

Although he was fatally wounded, Roberts still managed to get across the road and barricade himself in Dr. Blazer's house, where he found a rifle and continued firing on the Regulators. Brewer, determined to finish Roberts off, dodged behind a pile of logs directly across from where Roberts was holed up. Brewer fired at Roberts but missed. Roberts, however, noted the smoke in the air from Brewer's gun, and the next time Brewer stuck his head up from behind his shelter, Roberts fired, striking Brewer in the eye and blowing off the top of his head. In an instant, the fight changed. The Regulators, devastated by the loss of their leader, took their wounded men and left Roberts to die.

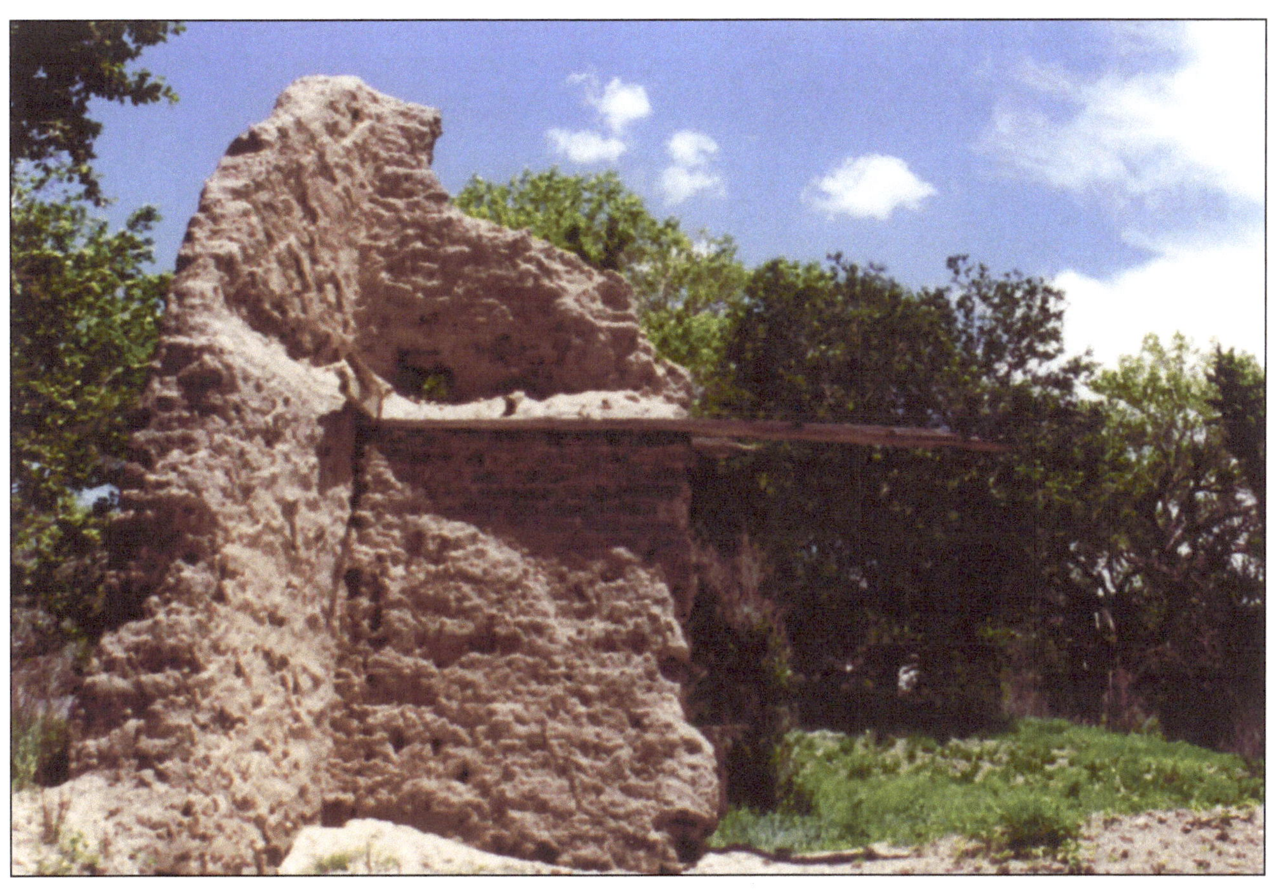

U.S. 70 now runs through the middle of what was once Blazer's Mill on the Mescalero Apache Indian Reservation. Few of the adobe structures that made up the mill remain.

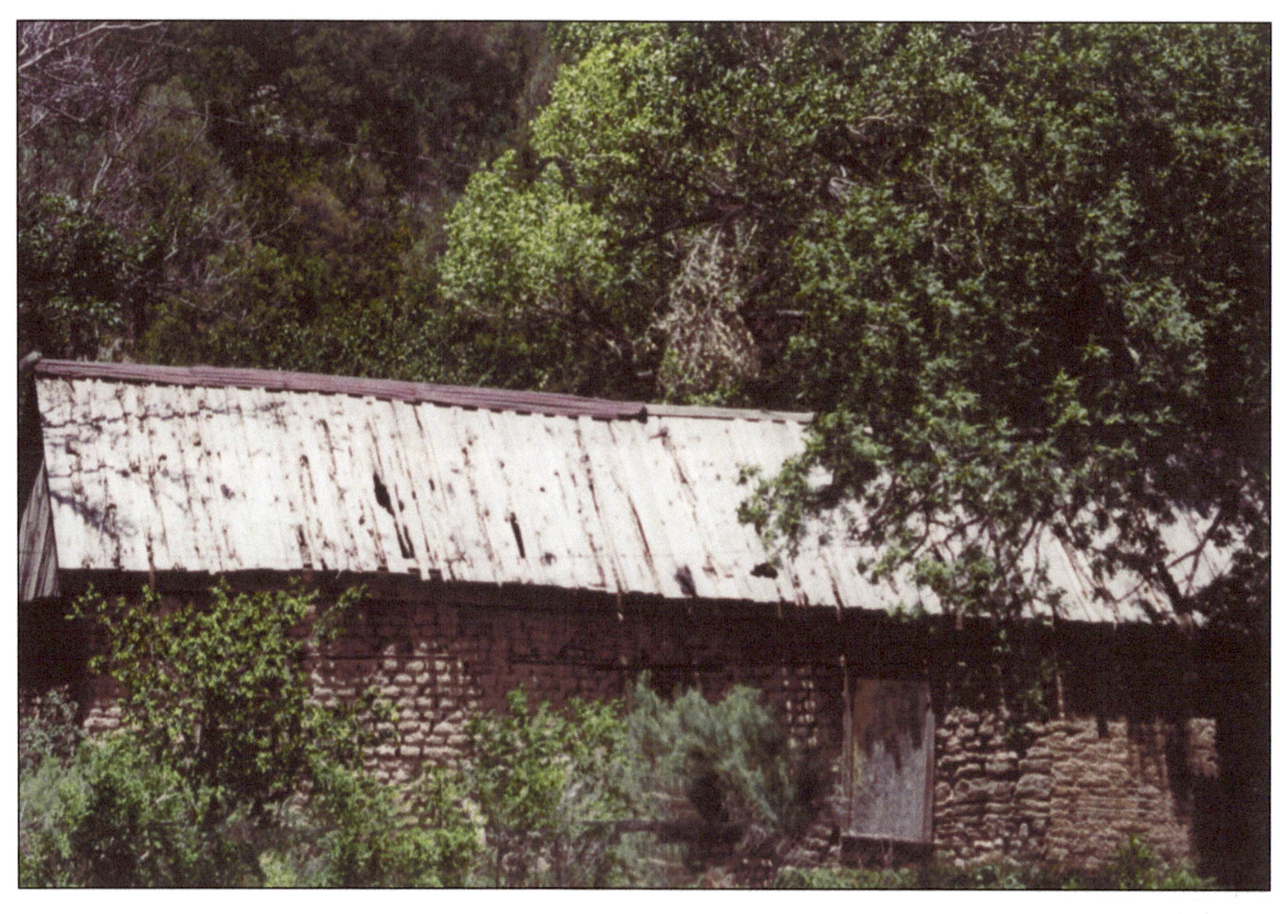

Across U.S. 70 from the adobe ruins stands what's believed to be the building in which Roberts barricaded himself.

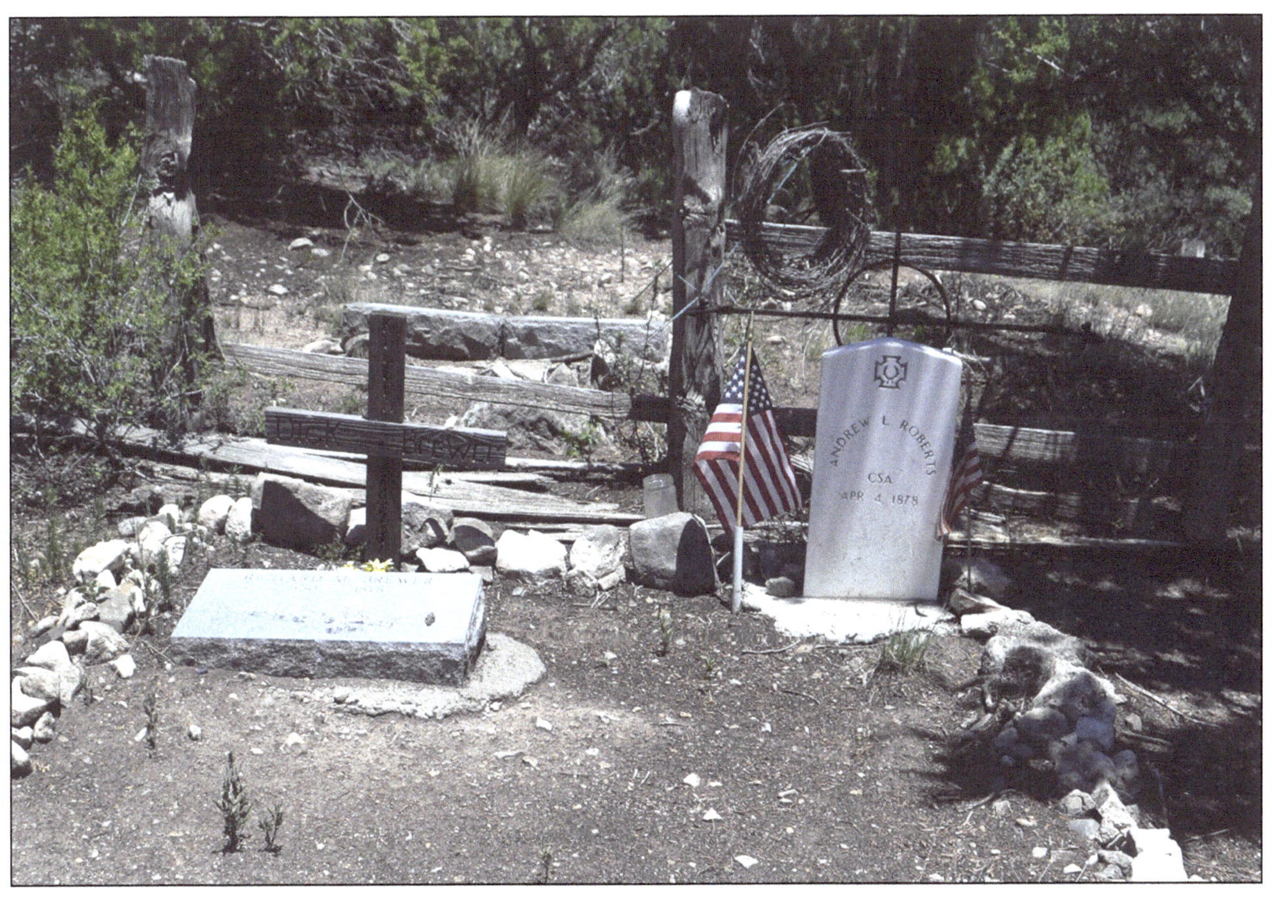

Dick Brewer and Buckshot Roberts were buried together in the Blazer family cemetery.

The Lincoln County War
Part II

Five months after the murder of John Tunstall, hostilities in Lincoln escalated into a full-blown battle between the Tunstall-McSween and Murphy-Dolan factions.

On Sunday, July 14, the Regulators rode into town to join the other McSween supporters for a fight. Charlie Bowdre, Doc Scurlock, Frank Coe, John Middleton, and ten others occupied the Ellis house on the east side of the single road that ran through town. Up the street, Martin Chavez led twenty native New Mexican volunteers in the Montaño and Patrón houses. George Coe, Henry Brown, and Sam Smith were stationed in the back of the Tunstall store, while next door with McSween in his home were Billy, his new sidekick Tom Folliard, Jim French, Yginio Salazar, José Chávez y Chávez, and about nine others. All in all, the McSween side boasted approximately sixty men—outnumbering the Murphy-Dolan side by roughly twenty men. Brady's replacement, Sheriff George Peppin, was on the west side of town in the Wortley Hotel with Dolan and over two dozen others, including Jesse Evans, Billy Mathews, and Jack Long. Dolan men were also across the street at the House and stationed in the torreón, located in the middle of town between the Tunstall store and Montaño house.

The first move was made on Monday when Dolan sent Peppin and Long to McSween's home with arrest warrants for Billy and several others. Their demands for surrender were answered with a hail of gunfire. On Tuesday, Dolan sent word to Lt. Col. Dudley at nearby Fort Stanton asking to borrow a howitzer. Although Dudley was a Murphy-Dolan sympathizer, he couldn't grant the request because it was a civilian matter. That changed, however, when the soldier carrying Dudley's reply accused someone on the McSween side of shooting at him.

The next day, Dudley sent soldiers to investigate the alleged shooting, but no attempts to arrest anyone were made. On Thursday, there was a rumor that John Chisum was sending another thirty-five men to aid McSween. If this was true, they didn't arrive before all hell broke loose.

On Friday, July 19, Dudley decided to bring troops into Lincoln under the guise of protecting the women and children. But rather than locate any women or children, Dudley set up his camp directly across the street from the Montaño and Patrón houses and aimed both a Gatling gun and a howitzer at the McSween men. Facing the threat of Army weapons, the men inside the two buildings retreated down the street to the Ellis house. This effectively caused the men in the McSween house and Tunstall store to be surrounded by Dolan forces on either side—the soldiers and the men in the torreón to the east and the men in the Wortley and the House to the west. There was no hope for an easy escape.

Later that day, Susan McSween, still in her home with her sister and her sister's five children, braved the street and marched down to Dudley's camp to demand his protection. After arguing with Dudley, who refused to listen, Susan returned to her home in time to see Long and another of Peppin's men setting fire to the kitchen. The fire was promptly extinguished, but when they tried again later that day, Dolan men fired at the McSween men, keeping them from putting out the flames. Soon after, the women and children were finally granted protection and escorted from the burning house.

The McSween's house was U-shaped and made of adobe. Fortunately, this meant the fire spread slowly, giving the men trapped inside time to make a plan. Taking charge, Billy decided the only way to escape was to try and sneak out at nightfall. He was sure they would be safe if they could make it to the Rio Bonito behind the house.

When darkness fell, Billy, Folliard, Chávez y Chávez, and French sneaked out, hoping to draw enemy fire so McSween and the others could get away safely. But the fire from the house burned bright, and they were quickly spotted. When the shooting began, Billy, a gun in each hand, fired into the darkness and escaped. McSween, however, was tired of fighting and called out, "I shall surrender." He was killed immediately. Dubbed "The Big Kill," the death of McSween during the Five-Day Battle marked the end of the Lincoln County War. With the war over, Billy started his new life as an outlaw.

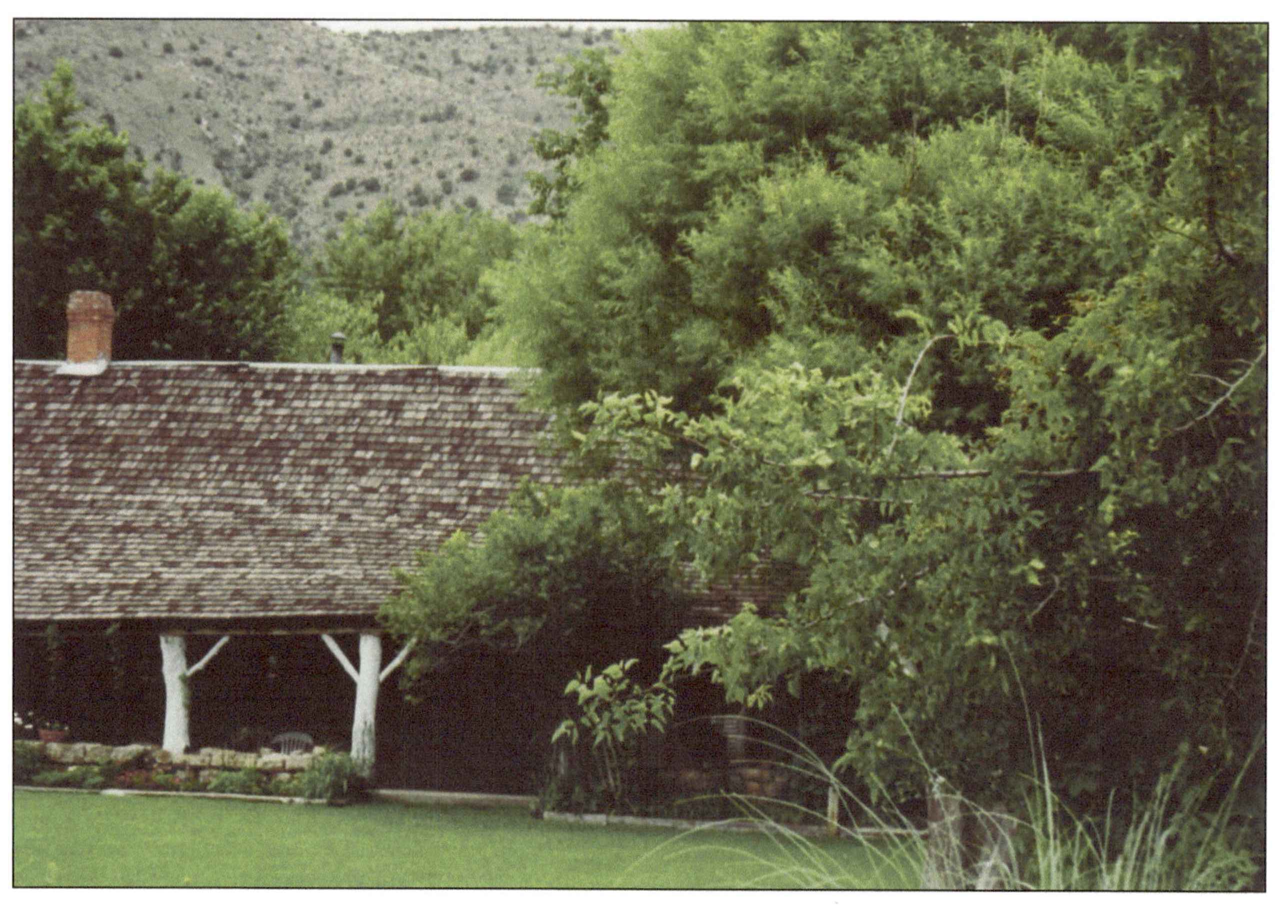

The Ellis house

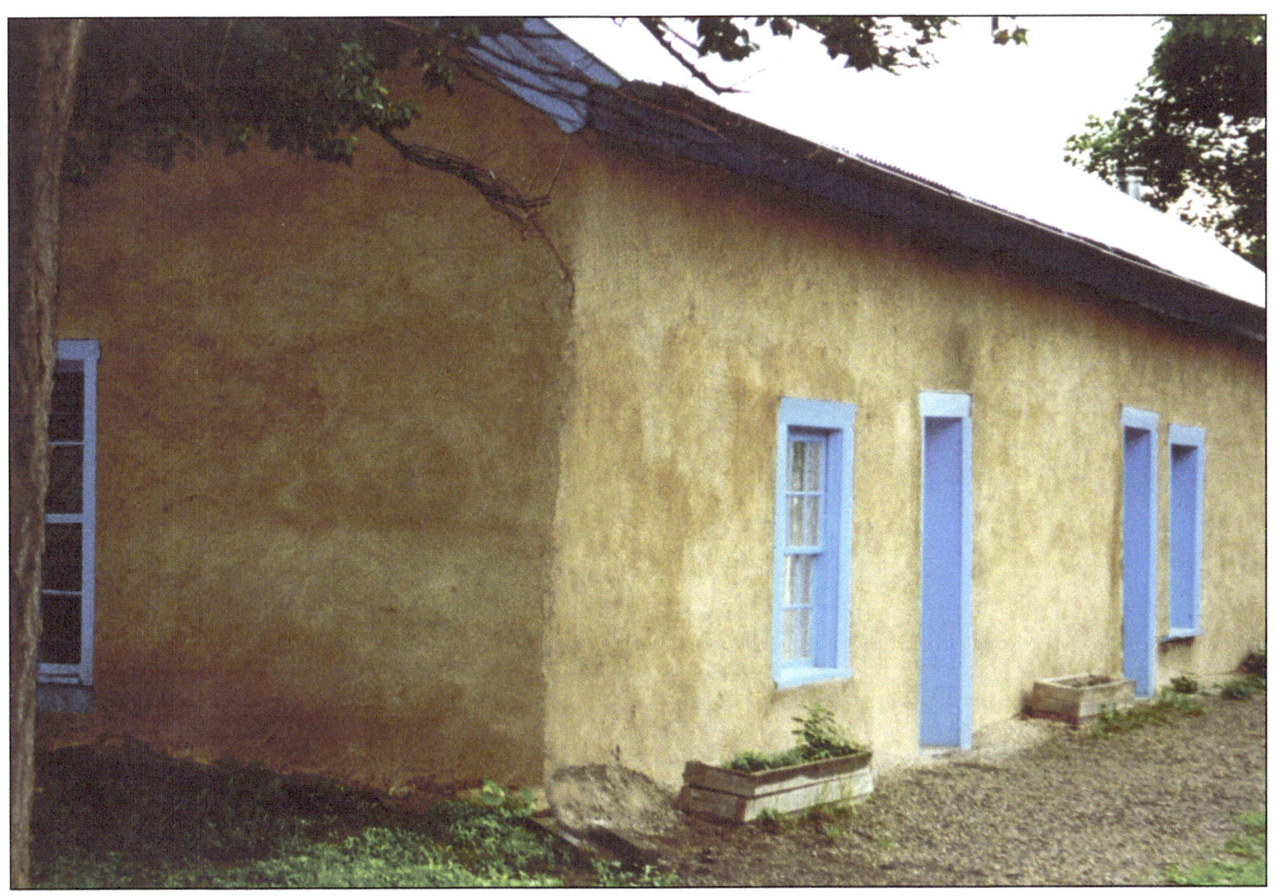

The Montaño house

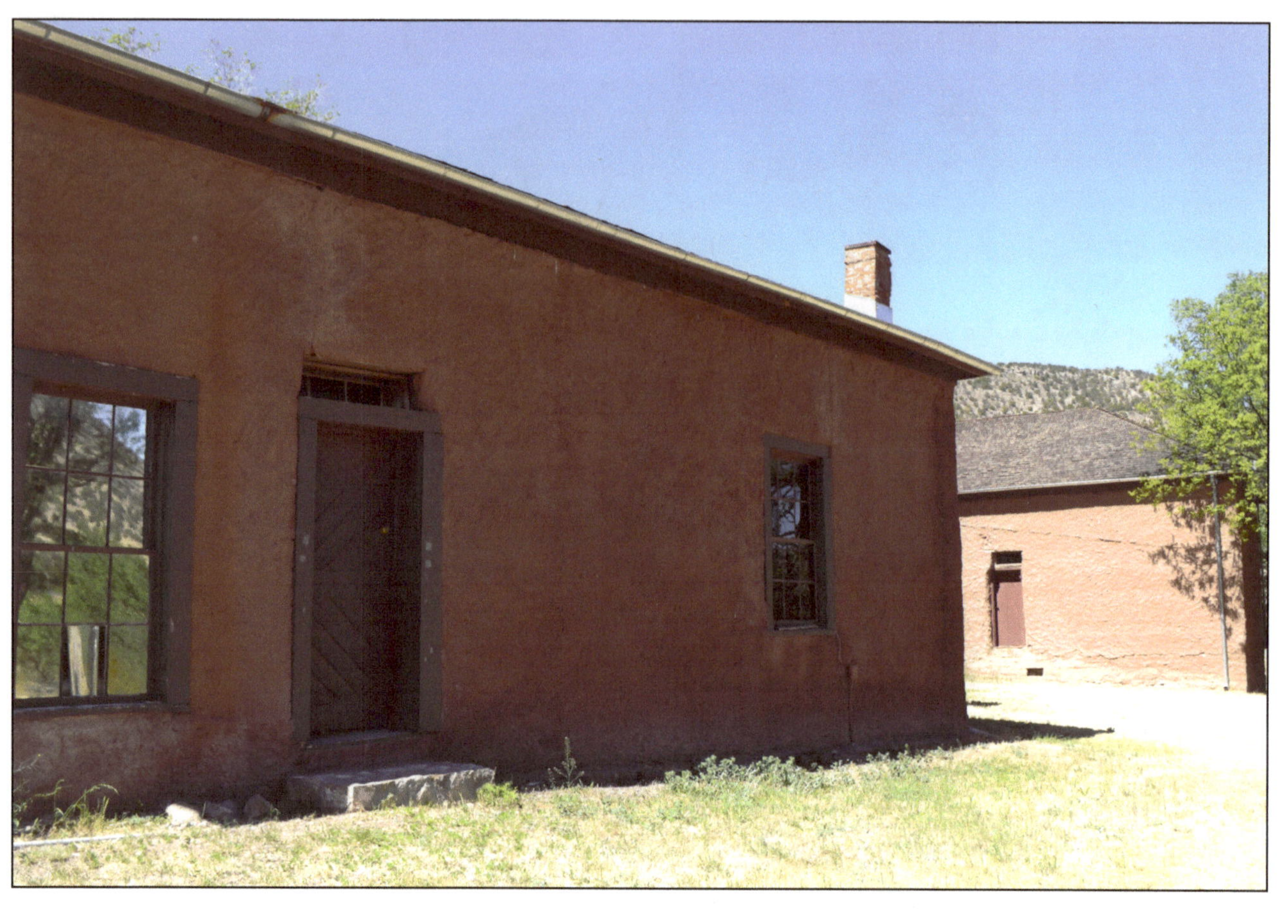

Behind the Tunstall store

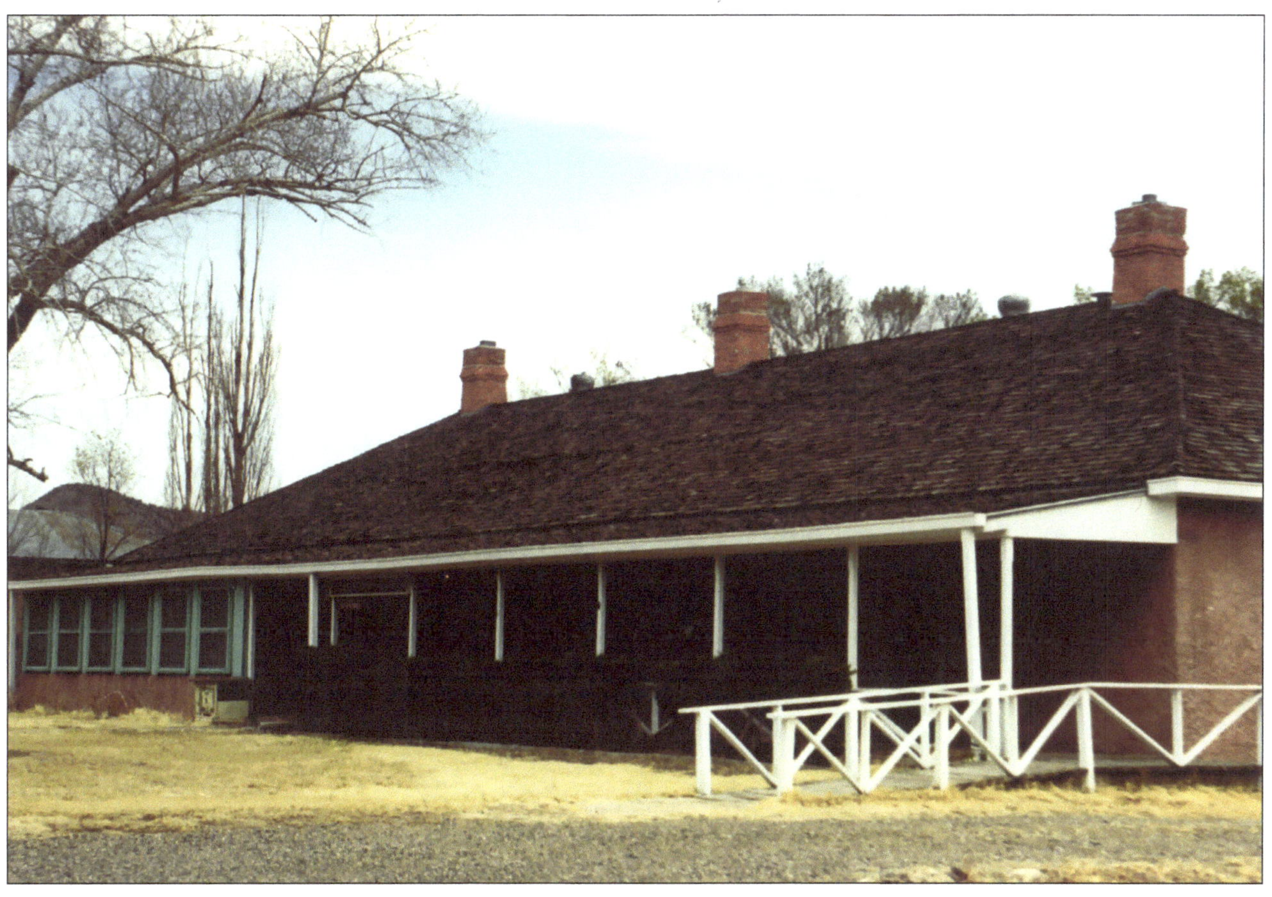

The Wortley Hotel

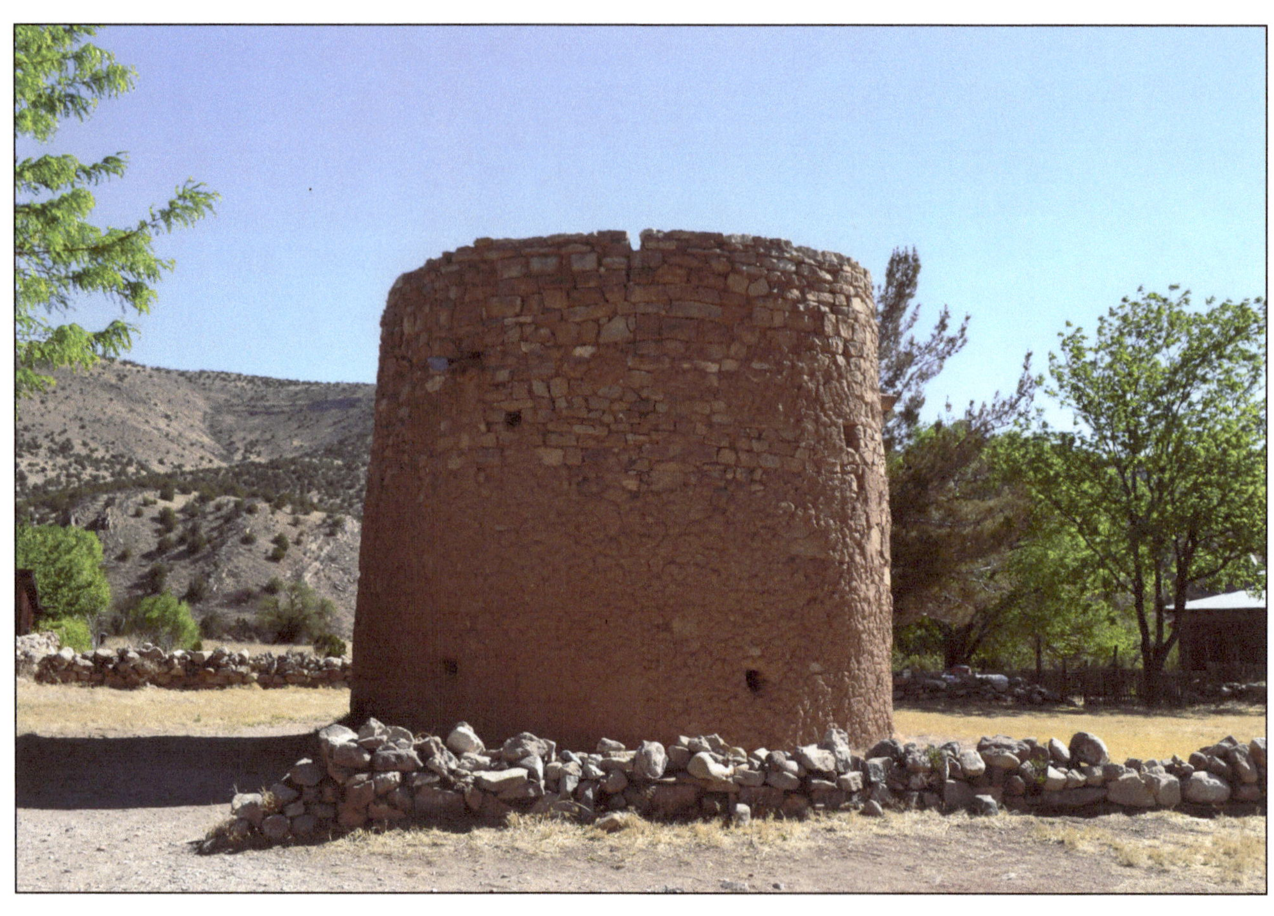

El Torreón, a stone structure once used against raiding Apaches

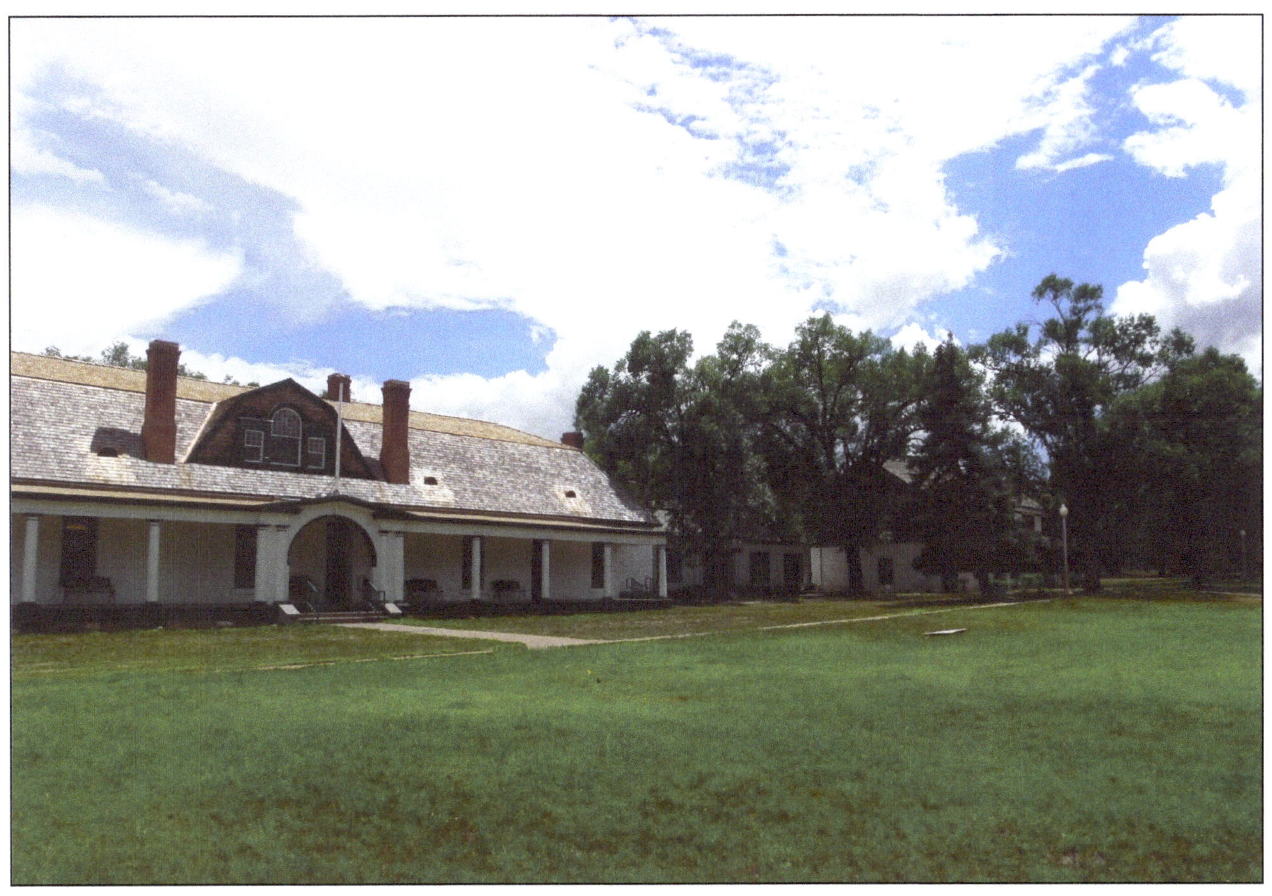

Fort Stanton

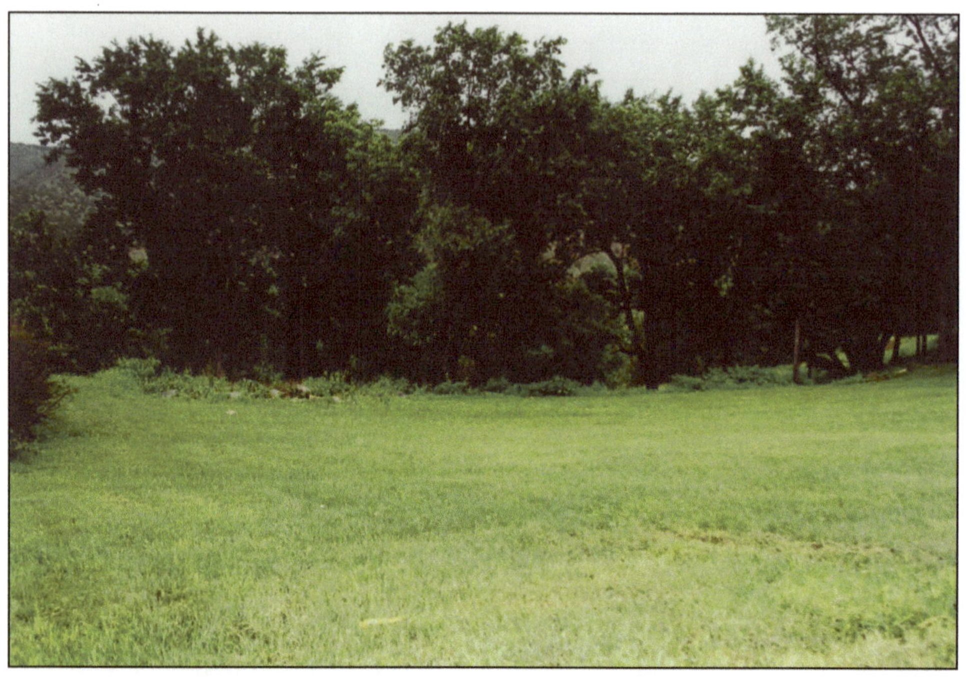

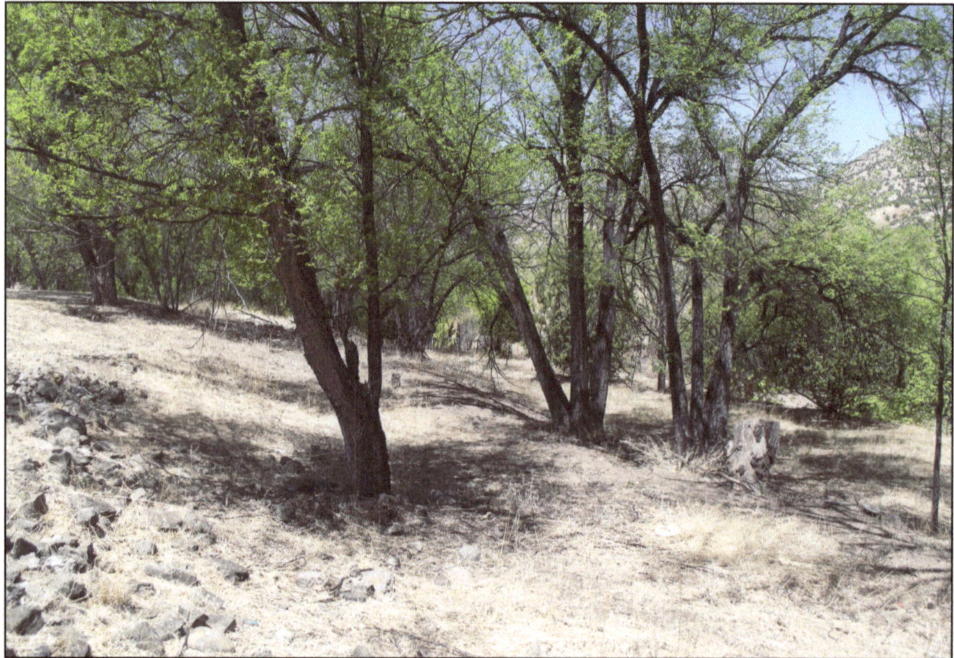

Top: The site of McSween's house. After it burned it was never rebuilt.

Bottom: The Regulator's escape route to the Rio Bonito behind McSween's house

Opposite Page: McSween's grave marker next to Tunstall's

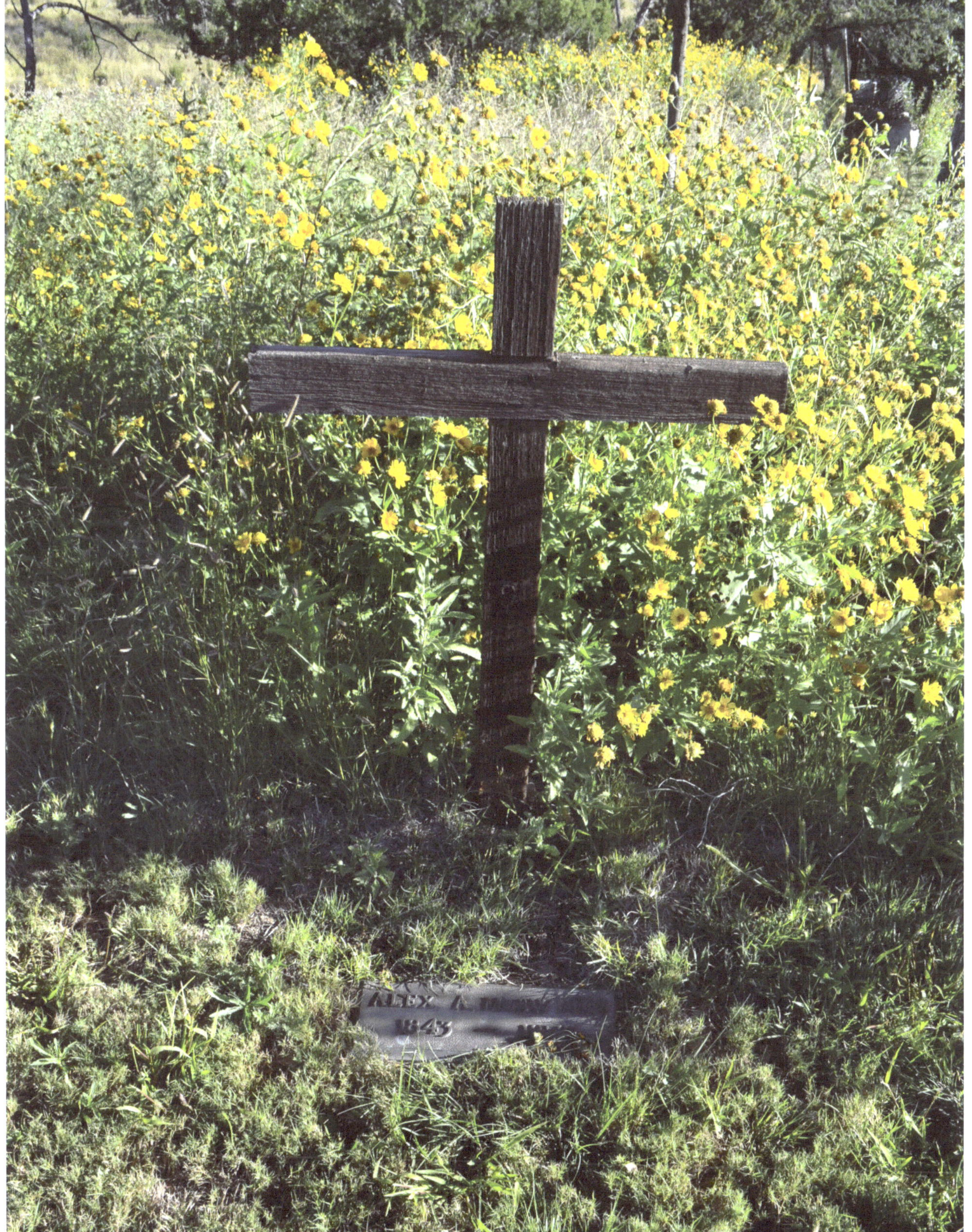
ALEX A.
1843

On the Run

After escaping from Lincoln, many Regulators made their way north to the towns along the Pecos River. Some, like Charlie Bowdre and Doc Scurlock, decided to settle down in Fort Sumner and started working for the Maxwell family. Others, like the Coe cousins, decided to leave New Mexico altogether. But Billy, unwilling to stay out of trouble, declared he would remain in New Mexico and "steal [himself] a living." So, Billy and the rest of the like-minded Regulators spent much of the next few months making friends with the locals, attending dances, gambling, rustling, and dodging the law.

Although Billy's life during this time was that of a nomad, of all the towns he frequented, Fort Sumner was probably the closest thing to a home he had. Union forces built the fort in 1862 when Kit Carson forced thousands of Navajo and Apache Indians to leave their land and live on the nearby reservation. In 1868, the captives were sent home, and the fort was abandoned until 1871, when land baron and rancher Lucien B. Maxwell purchased it. Maxwell turned the army barracks into living quarters that housed many permanent and temporary residents.

It was here that Billy befriended a bartender named Pat Garrett and struck up a romance with Lucien Maxwell's daughter Paulita—both of whom would come to play an important role in his life.

In the meantime, while Billy and his friends were across the border in Tascosa, Texas, selling off a large herd of stolen horses, Susan McSween was in Lincoln preparing for a new battle against Lt. Col. Dudley for his part in the death of her husband. It was another war Billy would be pulled into.

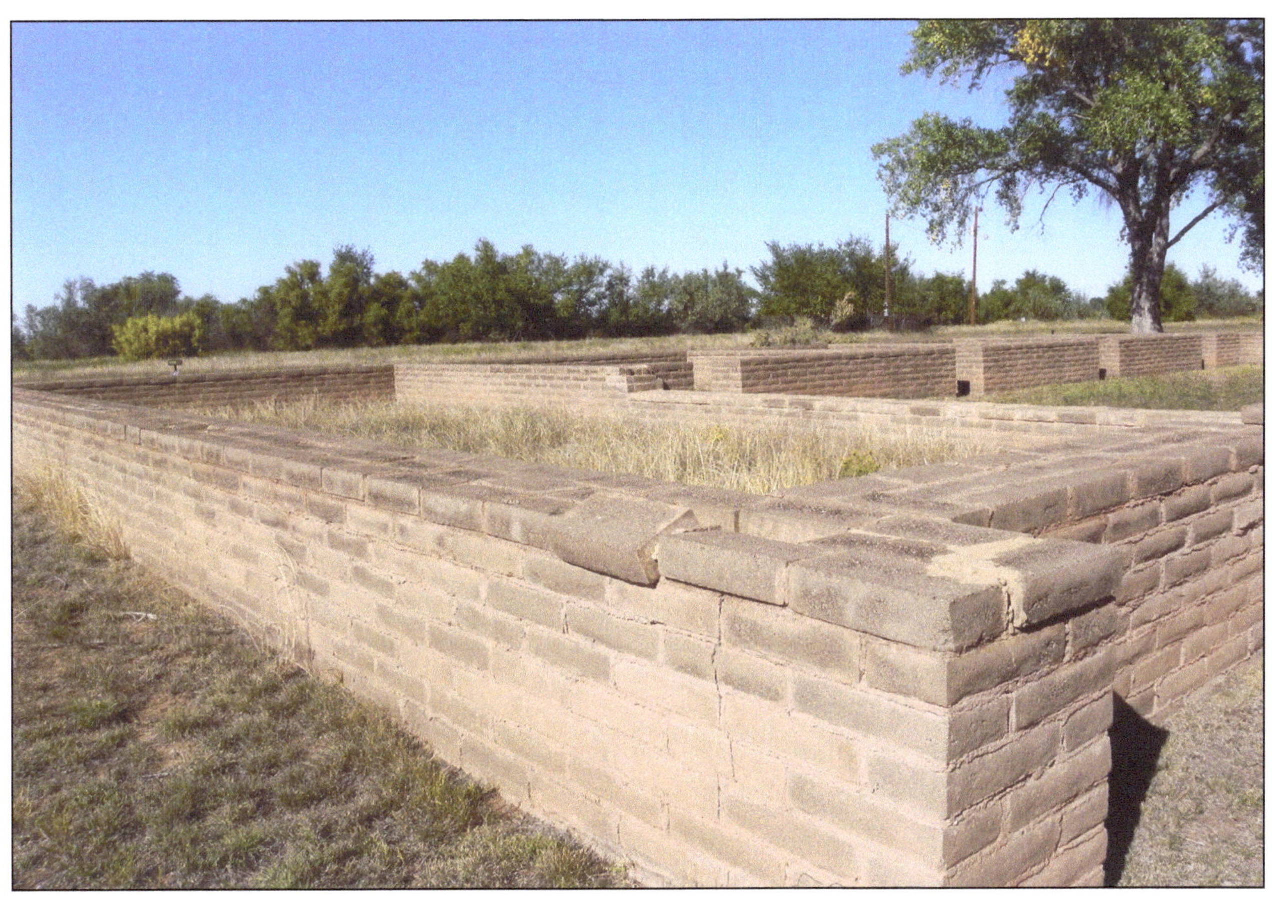

Over the years, Fort Sumner's buildings were lost due to flooding of the Pecos River. Today, what stands is a reconstruction of the barrack walls over the original site.

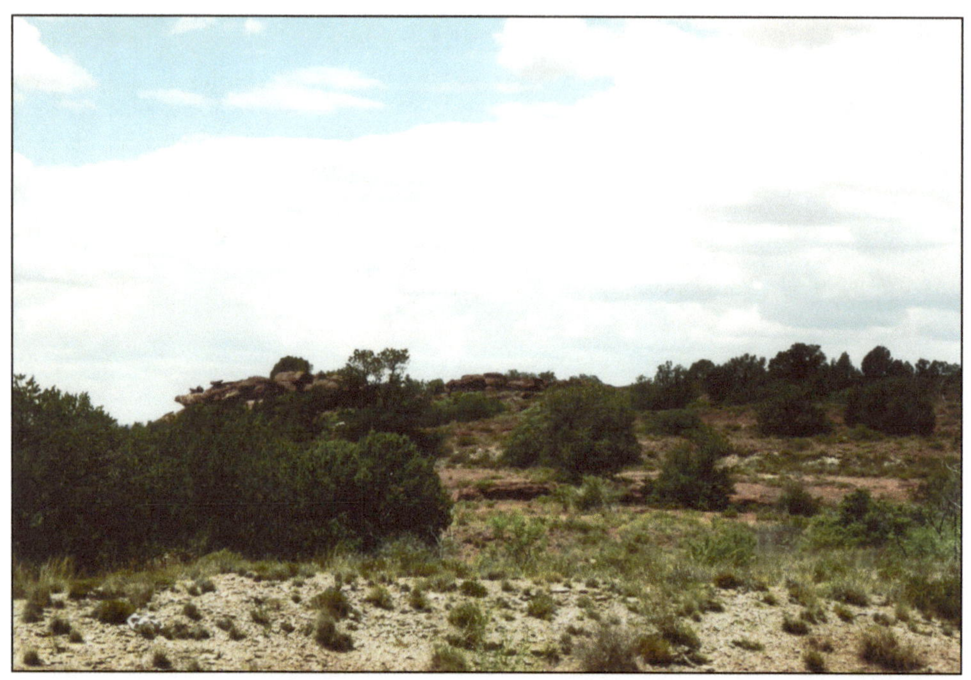

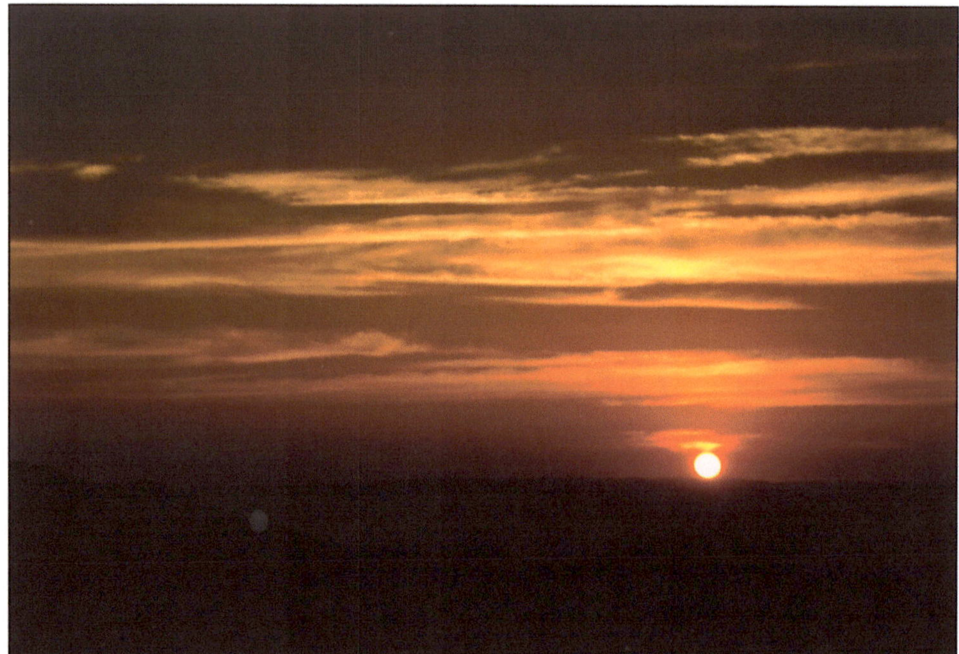

Top: Santa Rosa

Bottom: The road between Fort Sumner and Santa Rosa

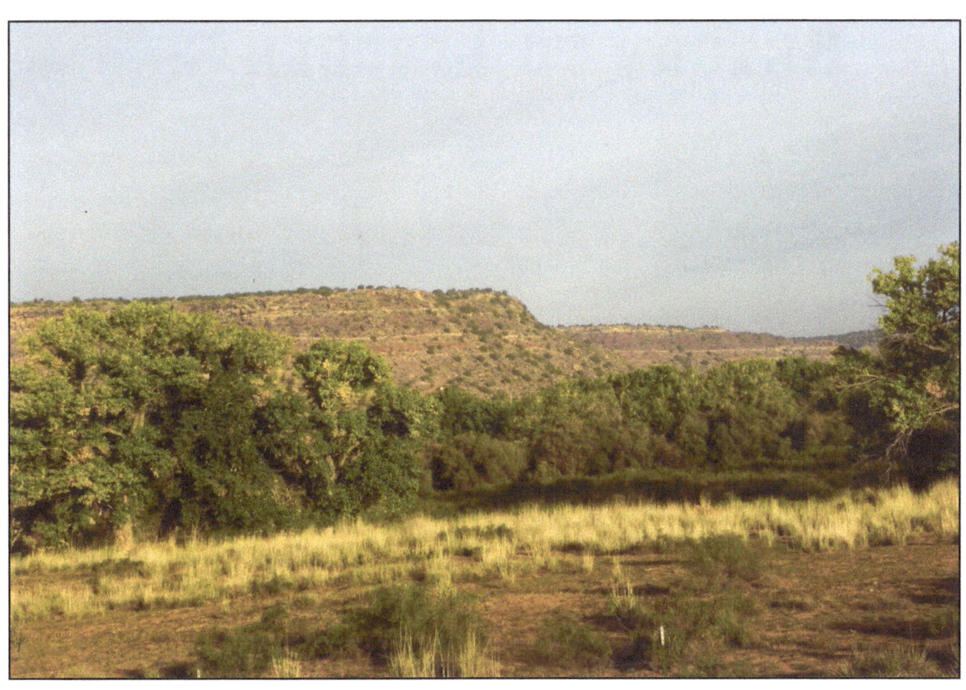

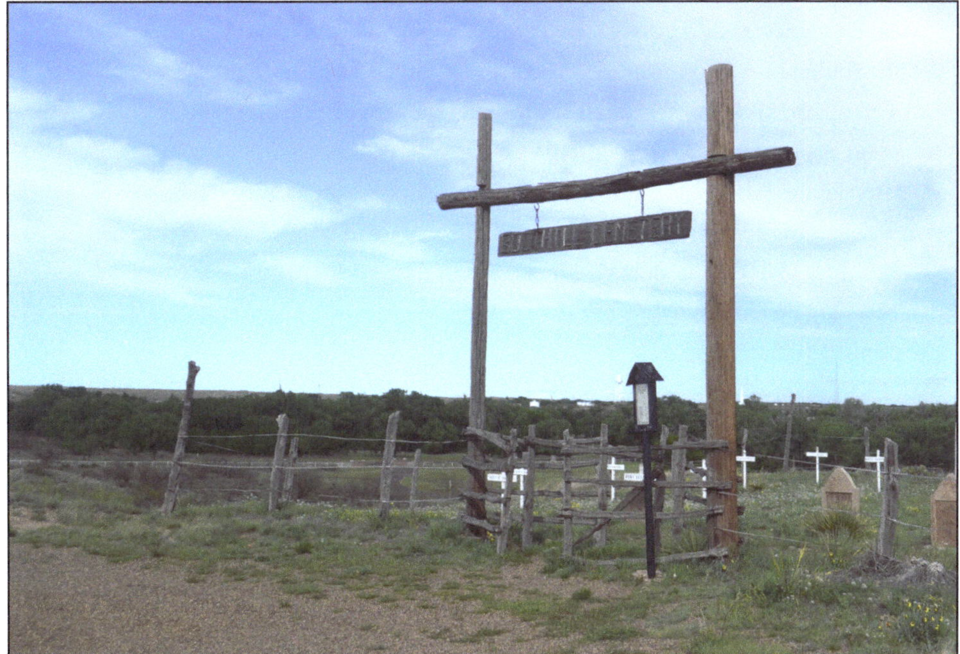

Top: The Pecos River Valley

Bottom: Tascosa, Texas

Return to Lincoln

In February of 1879, Billy once again returned to Lincoln. He may have been looking for help from Huston Chapman, Susan McSween's lawyer, who had just filed suit against Dudley for his actions—or lack thereof—during the Five-Day Battle. Tensions were still running high in the little town, and it was widely felt that Chapman was stirring up trouble. But by this time, Billy was tired of running from the law and was looking for a way out.

This might also have been the reason that on February 18, one year to the day that Tunstall was killed, a peace parley was arranged between the McSween and Dolan factions. Billy, Folliard, Scurlock, and two others on the McSween side agreed to meet with Dolan, Evans, Mathews, and Billy Campbell in a bar on the east side of town. Once the truce details were hashed out, the men started to celebrate. The Kid and Folliard watched as the others became drunk and violent but were powerless to stop them—nor could they refuse when the party moved to another bar.

Walking down the dark street, the group happened upon Chapman, who had just ridden into town. Campbell pulled his gun and started an argument with Chapman, and minutes later, both he and Evans simultaneously shot and killed the lawyer.

After killing Chapman, the men went into McCullum's Oyster House, where Dolan suggested someone place a gun in the dead man's hand so they could claim self-defense. Billy volunteered, but instead of planting the gun on Chapman, he and Folliard went down to the Ellis house, got their horses, and escaped to San Patricio.

Opposite Page Top: The site of Huston Chapman's murder

Opposite Page Bottom: The corral behind the Ellis house where Billy and Folliard had their horses

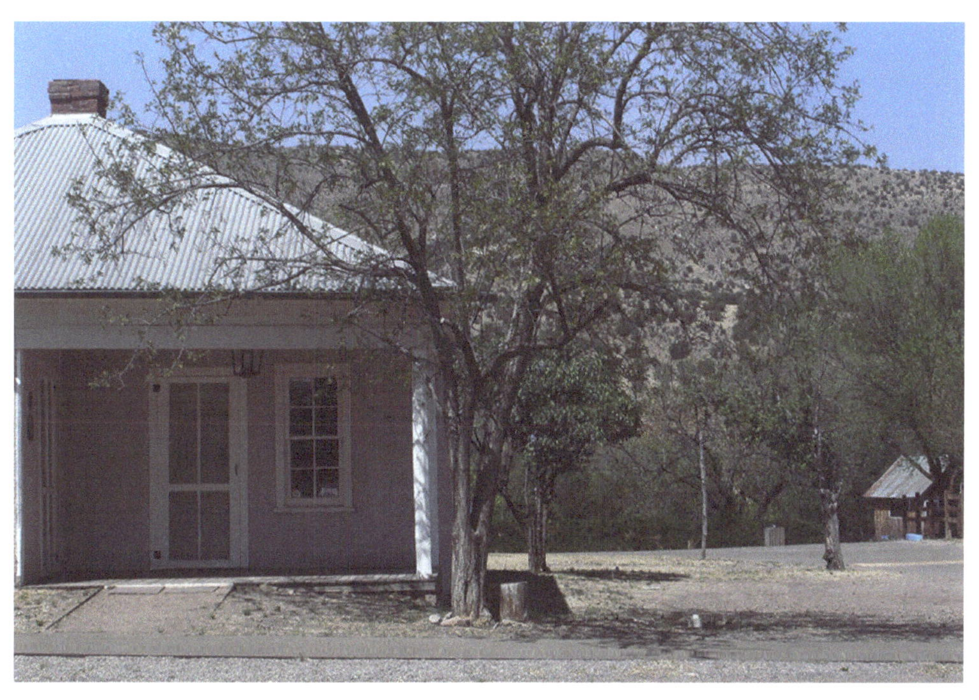

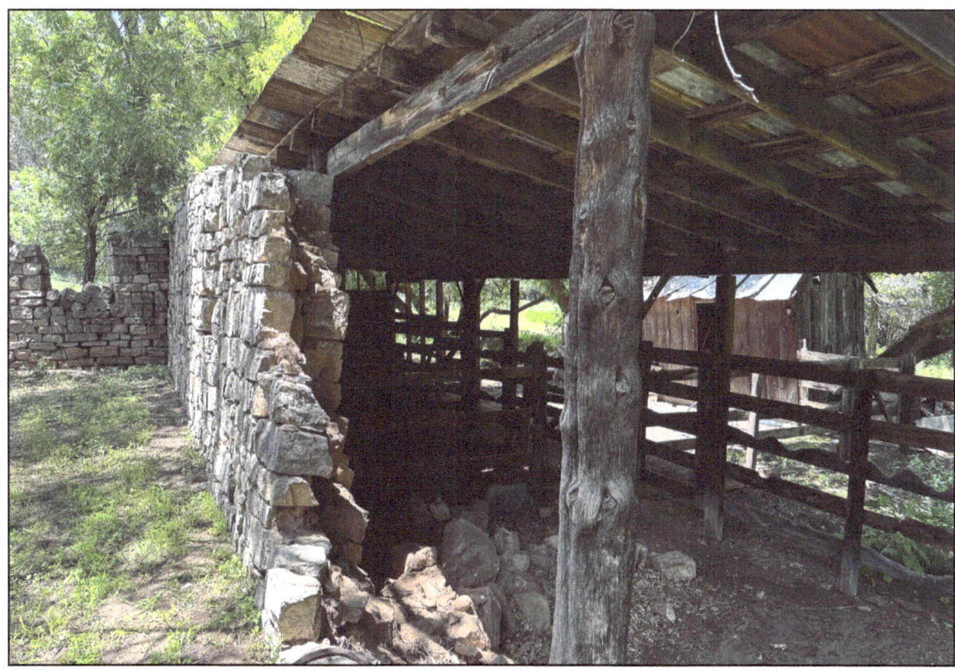

House Arrest

In September 1878, General Lew Wallace was appointed the new governor of New Mexico. Wallace was determined to fix the problems in the territory created by his corrupt predecessors and set his sights on Lincoln County. First, he suspended Dudley and set a court of inquiry. Next, he arrested Campbell, Evans, and Dolan for the murder of Chapman. Wallace also wanted the Kid and Folliard, but they proved harder to catch than the others.

Fortunately for Wallace, it was Billy who made the first move, writing to Wallace in secret saying he was a witness to Chapman's murder. Billy explained to the governor about the indictments he had against him for the murders of Buckshot Roberts and Sheriff Brady and how dangerous it would be to come forward and testify against the men who, just a few weeks before, he had made a peace treaty with. Wallace replied, telling Billy, "I have authority to exempt you from prosecution if you will testify to what you say you know," and set up a secret meeting at Squire Wilson's home in Lincoln.

Billy met with Wallace and agreed to testify and in turn, Wallace agreed to let Billy go, "scot-free with a pardon in [his] pocket." A few days later, Billy and Folliard let themselves be arrested in San Patricio and brought to the Patrón house, where they were held until the trial.

Billy did his part and testified against those involved in the Lincoln County War and Chapman's murder. Many on the Murphy-Dolan side, including Dudley, were indicted for their roles in the Five-Day Battle; Dolan, Evans, and Campbell were indicted for Chapman's murder.

Billy was likewise charged with the murder of Sheriff Brady and Buckshot Roberts, but by then, Wallace had gone back to Santa Fe without granting his pardon. Billy was left in the hands of District Attorney William Rynerson, Dolan's good friend. Rynerson managed to get a change of venue to Doña Ana County for Dolan, Dudley, and Billy's trials—a smart move since it was almost certain that in Doña Ana, where Dolan had allies, he would go free and Billy would be found guilty.

Even with this news, Billy still testified in Dudley's court of inquiry, hoping Wallace would come through for him. He didn't, and the court found in favor of Dudley. Billy didn't care much for these developments and finally realized he wasn't getting his pardon. So, before he could be taken to Doña Ana, Billy left. He told his guards, "Boys, I'm tired of this. Tell the general I'm tired," and with that he and Folliard walked out the door of the Patrón house and became fugitives once again.

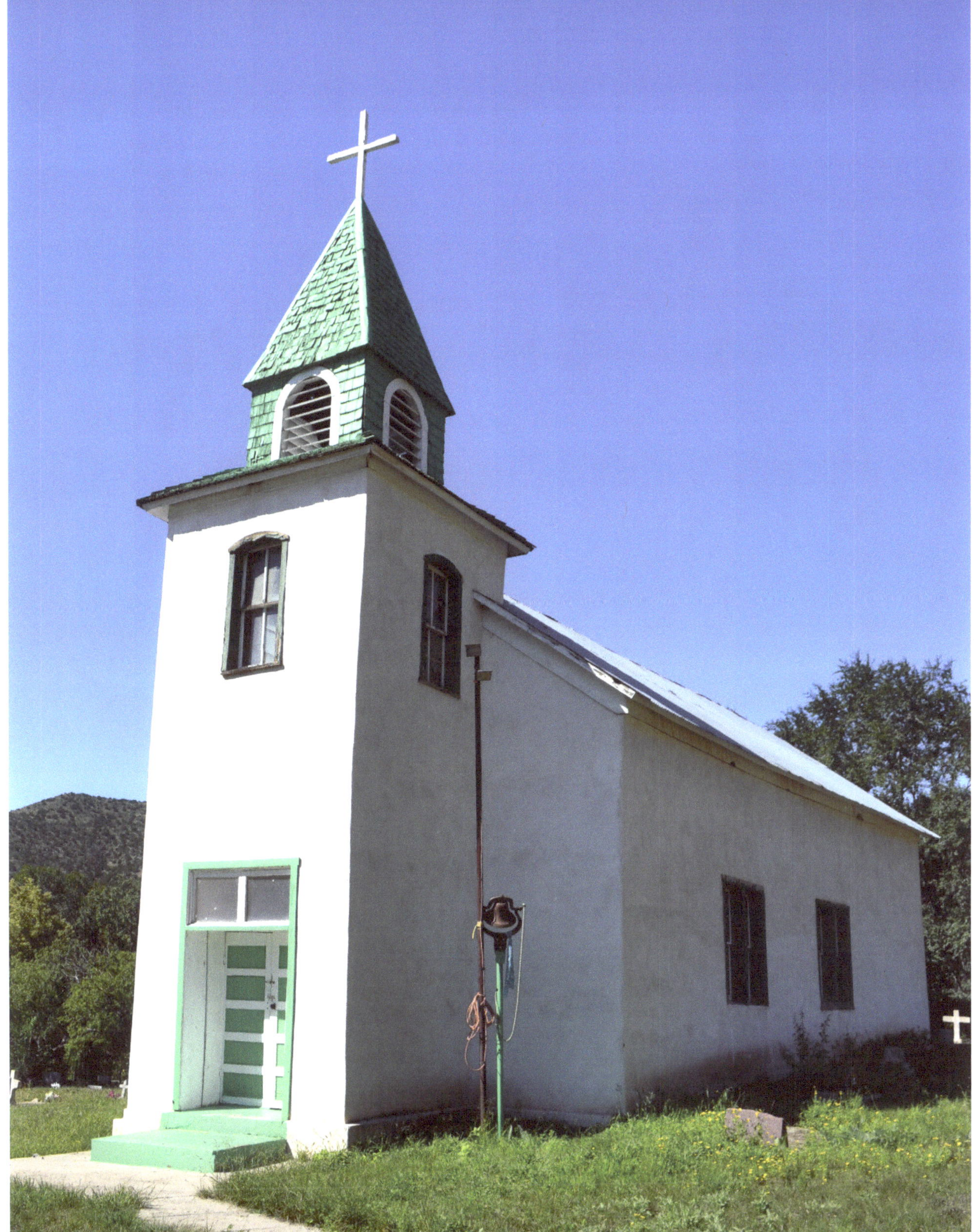

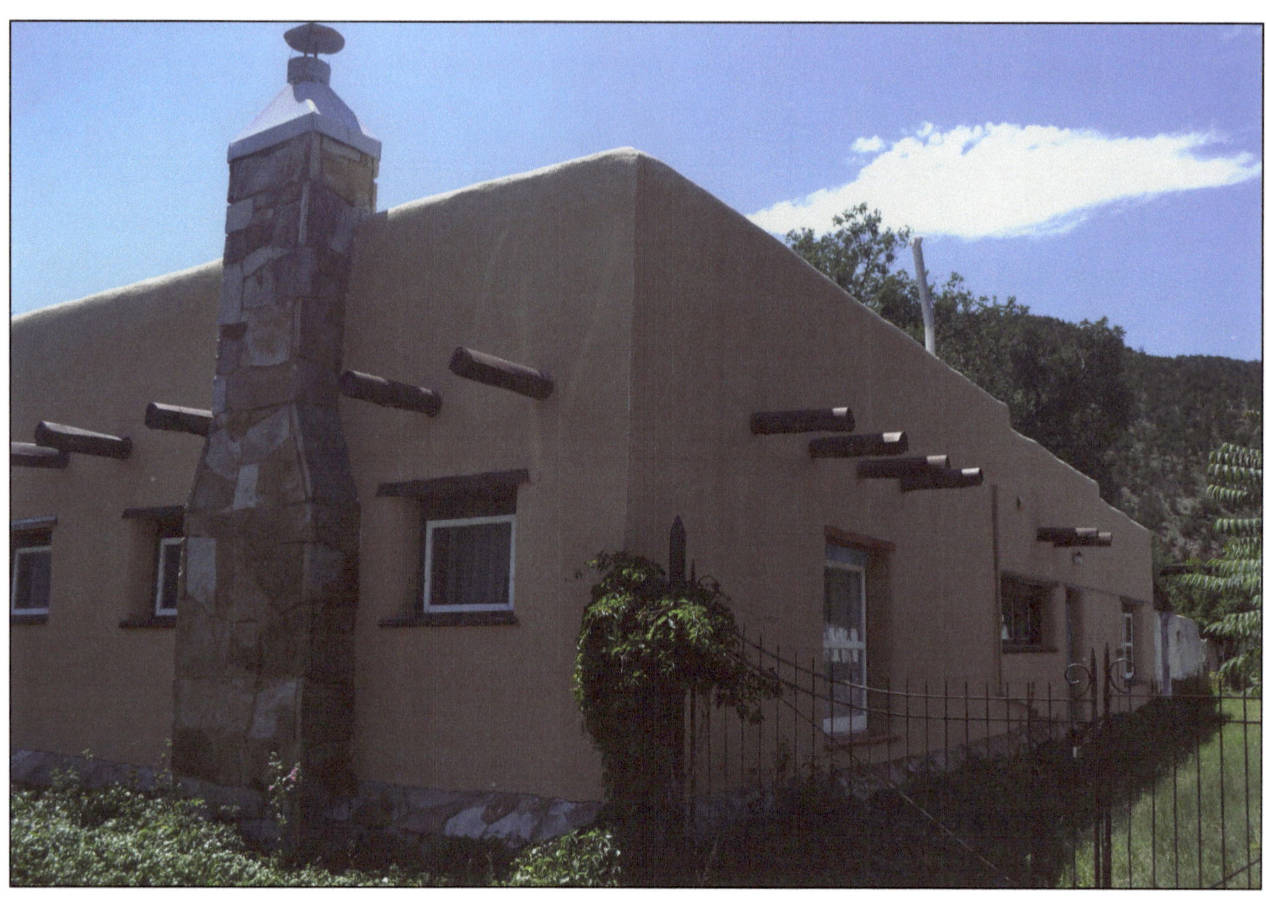

Previous Page: La Iglesia de San Patricio, built ca. 1875, a few years before Billy came to Lincoln County

Top: The Patrón house where, while under house arrest, Billy and Folliard were well fed, visited by friends, and serenaded at night by the locals under the front window; they were even allowed to take off their shackles when they were alone.

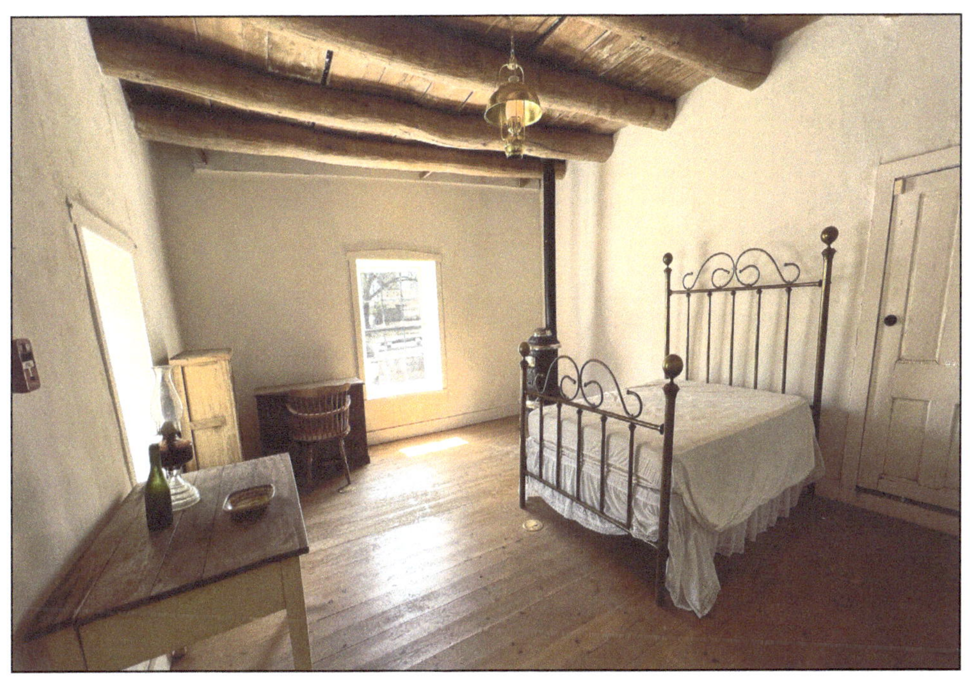

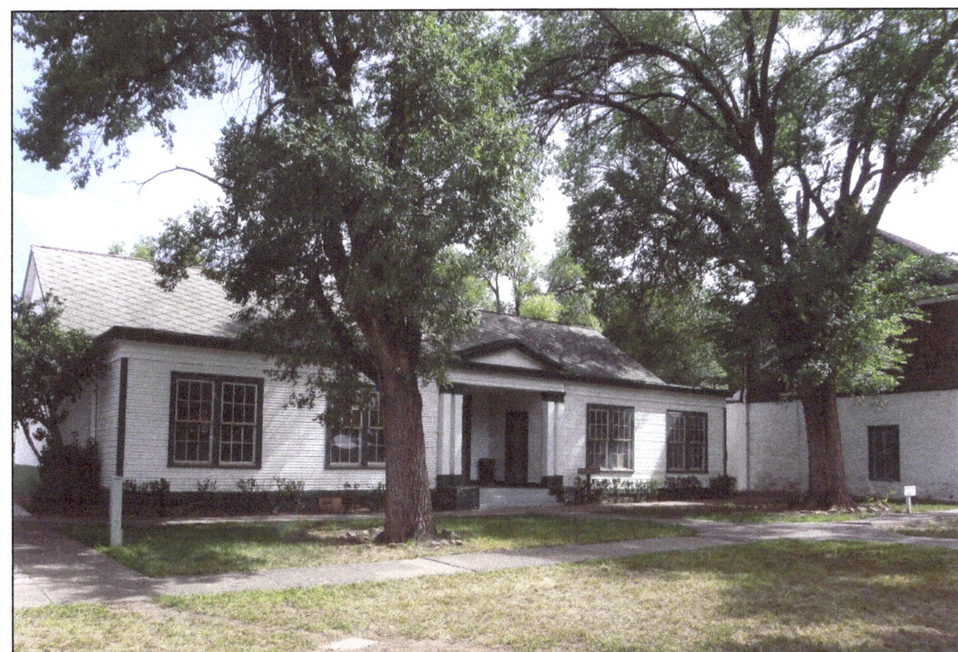

Top: The bedroom in the Montaño house where Lew Wallace stayed, directly next door to the Patrón house where he heard Billy being serenaded at night

Bottom: The guardhouse at Fort Stanton, where Billy and the others were held while they testified in the Dudley Court of Inquiry

Outlaw

Just as before, Billy spent the next few months roaming all over eastern New Mexico. He had friends throughout the territory that he could trust to keep his whereabouts a secret, and for over a year, he was able to avoid the law. Billy went to Las Vegas to stay at the hot springs and to see the trains; he visited Susan McSween in Lincoln; he gambled in White Oaks; and he danced with his sweethearts in Fort Sumner. And during all this, Billy found the time to rustle cattle and horses—mostly from John Chisum's herds because he believed Chisum owed him for his part in the Lincoln County War.

Meanwhile, Fort Sumner resident Pat Garrett married and moved to Roswell, hoping to become sheriff of Lincoln County. It was believed that Garrett had known Billy well enough during his time in Fort Sumner that he had an advantage in capturing the outlaw whose crimes (many of which were falsely attributed to him) were getting too numerous to ignore. Garrett won the election for sheriff on November 2, 1880, and was also appointed a deputy U.S. Marshal. Now, he not only had a warrant and the authority to arrest Billy the Kid, but Garrett also knew Billy's habits, his hiding places, and his friends.

Opposite Page: The San Jose Church in Anton Chico, where it's believed Pat Garrett married Apolonaria Gutiérrez in 1880—an event Billy may have attended

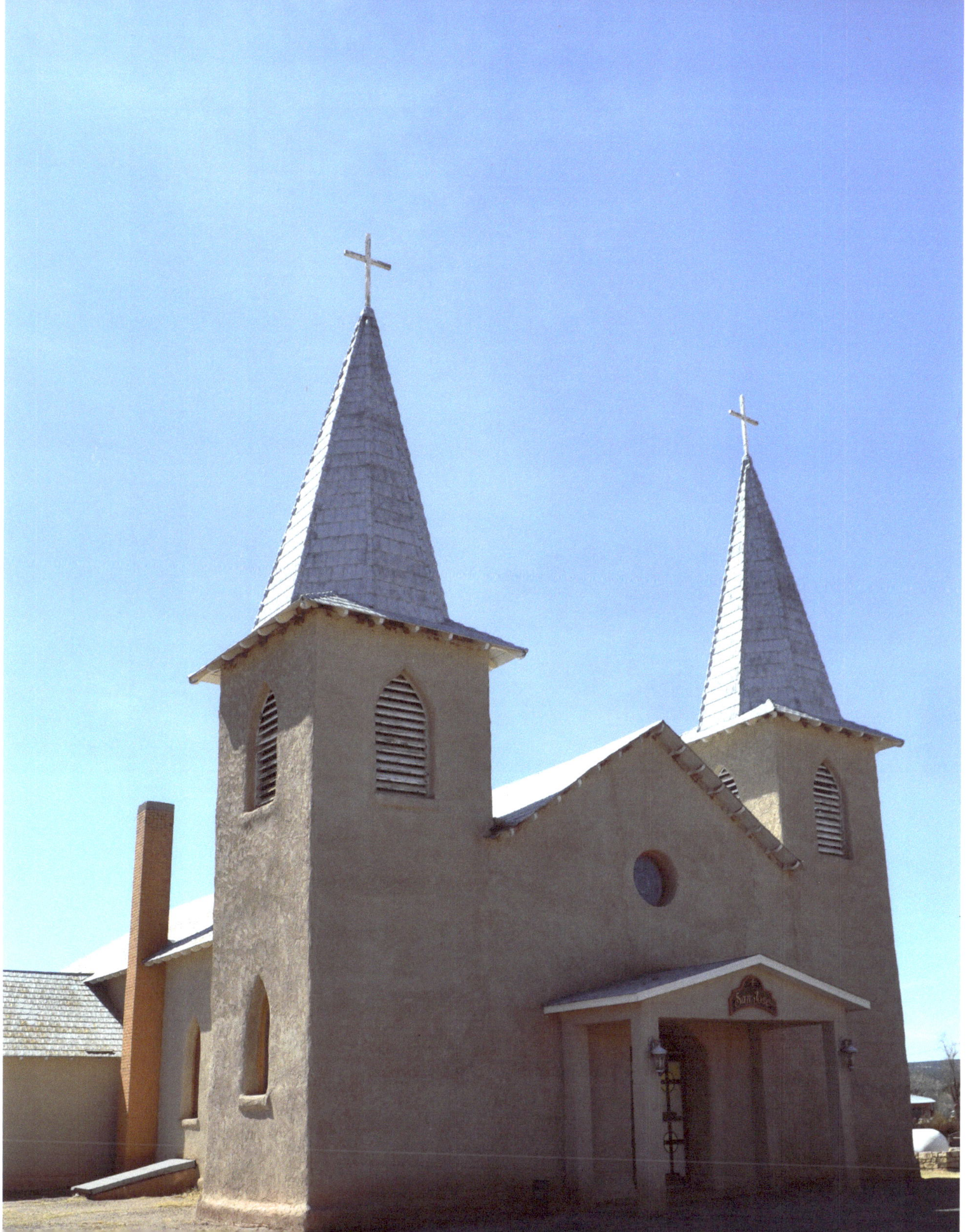

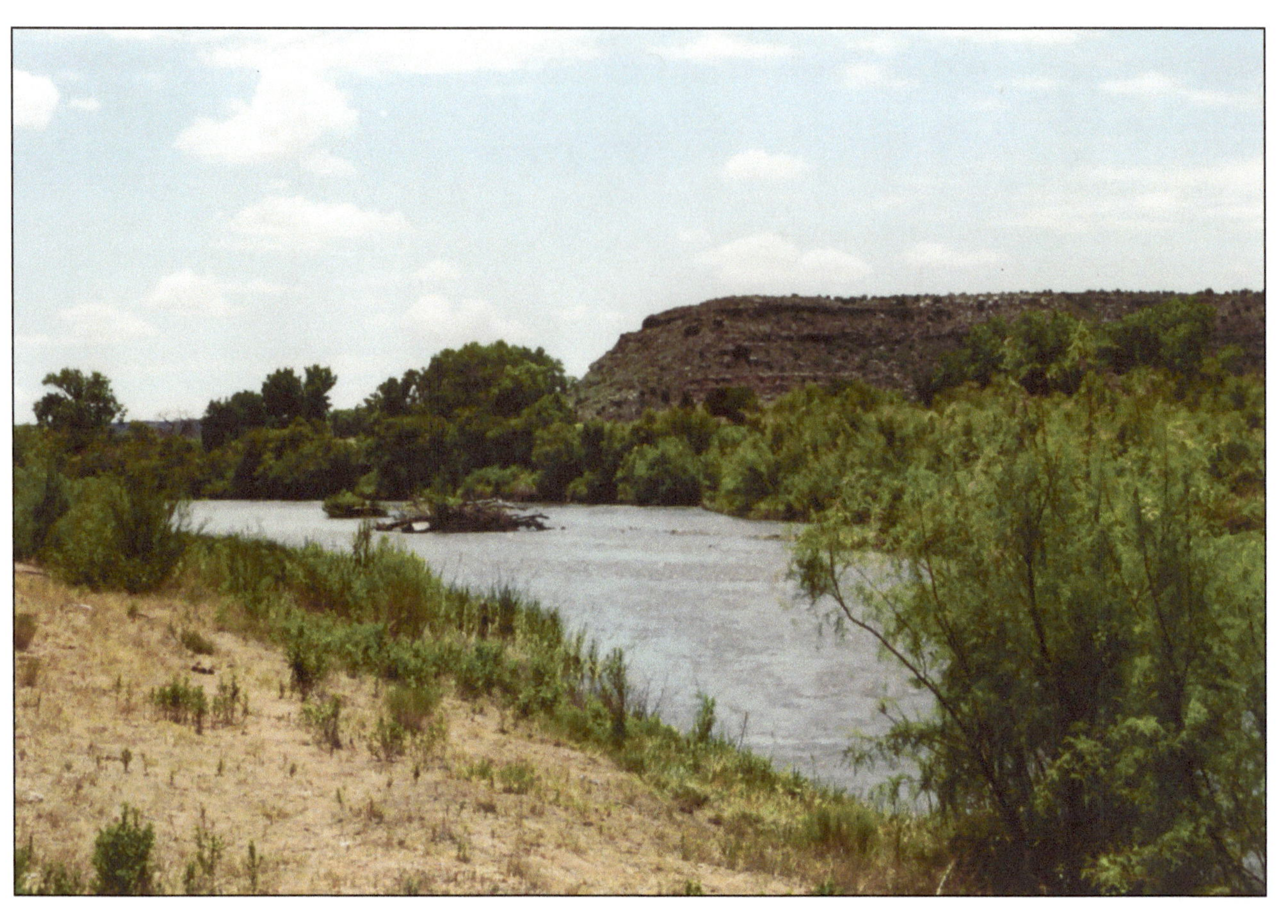

The Pecos River in Puerto de Luna

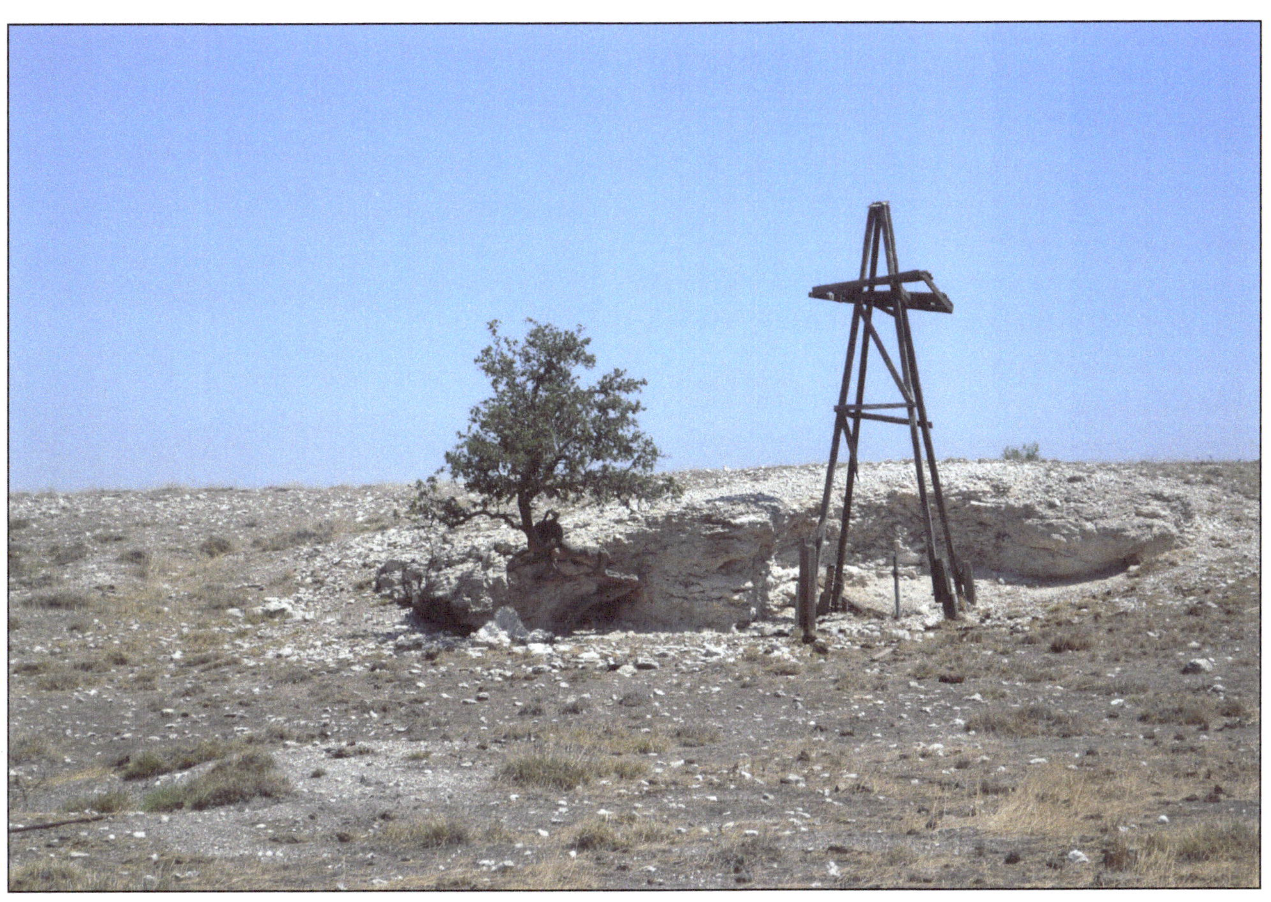

After Billy rustled cattle from the nearby ranches, he would graze them here at Portales Springs until he found buyers. The caves and the natural springs made it a perfect hideout.

White Oaks

While on the run from Garrett, Billy tried to meet with Ira Leonard, Susan McSween's new lawyer. He hoped Leonard could secure Wallace's promised pardon and attempted to meet him in White Oaks. Unfortunately, word of Billy's location spread, and soon, a posse made chiefly of anti-McSween men was formed to catch the outlaw.

On November 27, 1880, the White Oaks posse, led by James Carlyle, cornered Billy and his men at the Greathouse stage stop about thirty miles north of White Oaks. Billy's men exchanged notes with the posse outside, who were demanding they surrender. Billy refused, and Carlyle agreed to go inside to talk if Jim Greathouse would be a hostage for his men outside. After a few hours, Carlyle realized that talking to Billy was futile, that he was stalling and would never surrender. But Billy refused to let Carlyle go, and the men outside became restless. They threatened to kill Greathouse, so Billy warned that if a shot were fired, he would immediately kill Carlyle. Unfortunately, one of the men outside accidentally fired his gun due to having numb fingers from the cold. According to the Kid's account, Carlyle assumed Greathouse had been killed and panicked. Before Billy had a chance to retaliate against the presumed death of Greathouse, Carlyle leaped through the window only to be shot at by his own men, thinking he was Billy trying to escape. Both parties started to fire on each other, but Billy and his men managed to escape.

Not long after, newspapers pinned the blame for Carlyle's death on Billy. He wrote to Governor Wallace with his version of events and insisted he was innocent, that it was members of the White Oaks posse who killed Carlyle. Nevertheless, Wallace listened to public opinion over Billy's account and issued a $500 reward for the Kid's capture.

Opposite Page Top: According to a few old-timers, this is the possible remains of the White Oaks jail.

Opposite Page Bottom: Present-day Corona, the area where the Greathouse stage stop stood

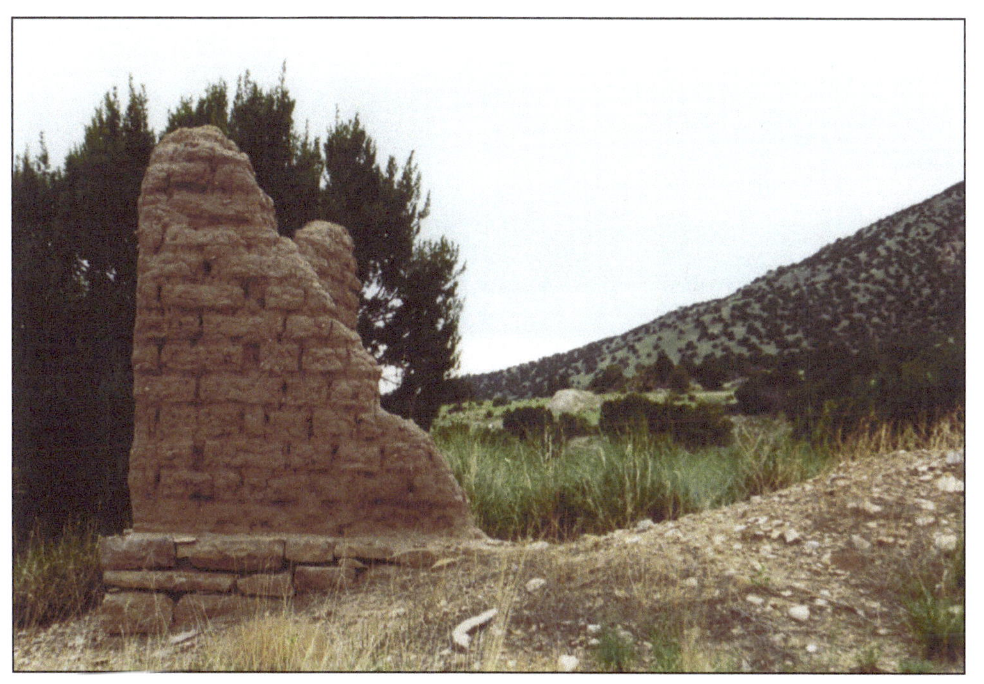

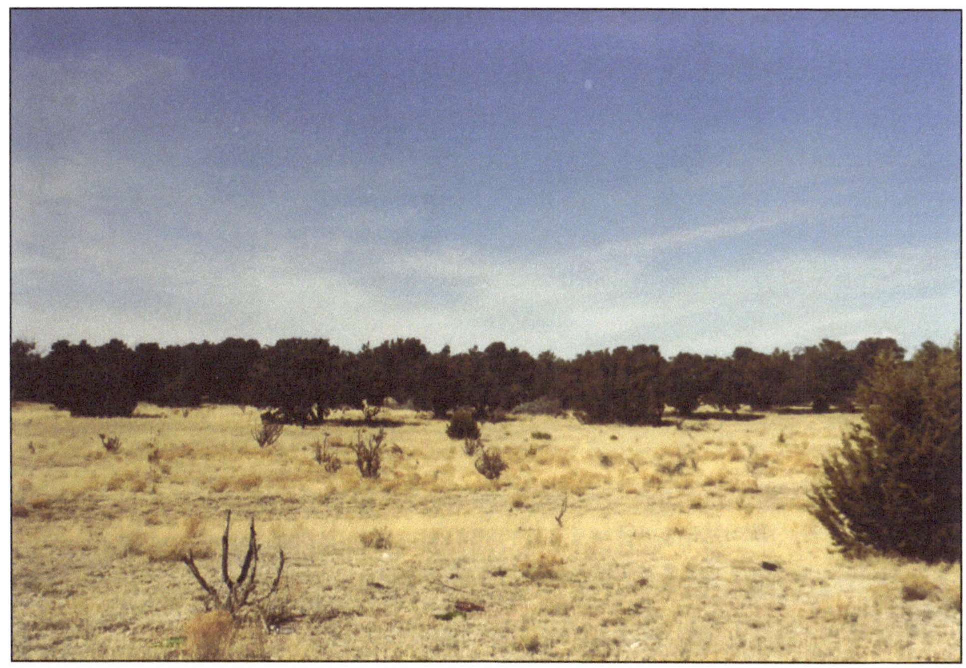

Capture

After the incident with Carlyle, Garrett formed another posse to track the Kid. He had it on good authority that Billy, Bowdre, Folliard, and a few newer members of the gang, Dave Rudabaugh, Tom Picket, and Billy Wilson, were close to Fort Sumner. Garrett and his men hid out in the old Indian hospital—the same building where Bowdre and his wife lived—and waited for Billy.

At about eleven o'clock on the night of December 19, Billy and the others rode into Fort Sumner and emerged from a veil of thick fog only to be spotted by Garrett's lookout. Garrett called out, telling the outlaws to throw up their hands; they responded with gunfire. Folliard was shot and killed in the chaos, but Billy and the others escaped.

Four days later, Garrett tracked the Kid and the others to a small stone house in Stinking Springs late at night. His men waited until daylight to verify that it was indeed Billy they had cornered. Wearing Billy's distinctive sugarloaf-style hat, Bowdre emerged from the house at dawn to feed the horses. Thinking it was Billy, Garrett demanded that he surrender. But before Bowdre could reply, the posse fired and killed him.

Still unwilling to surrender, the outlaws attempted to pull one of the horses inside, hoping to make a break for it. But Garrett shot and killed the horse, knowing that Billy's bay mare was inside with him and that it wouldn't cross the dead horse in the doorway. Garrett again demanded they surrender, but Billy remained stubborn and refused. It wasn't until the posse started to cook food that the hungry men inside the stone house gave themselves up. On December 23, 1880, the infamous Billy the Kid was finally captured.

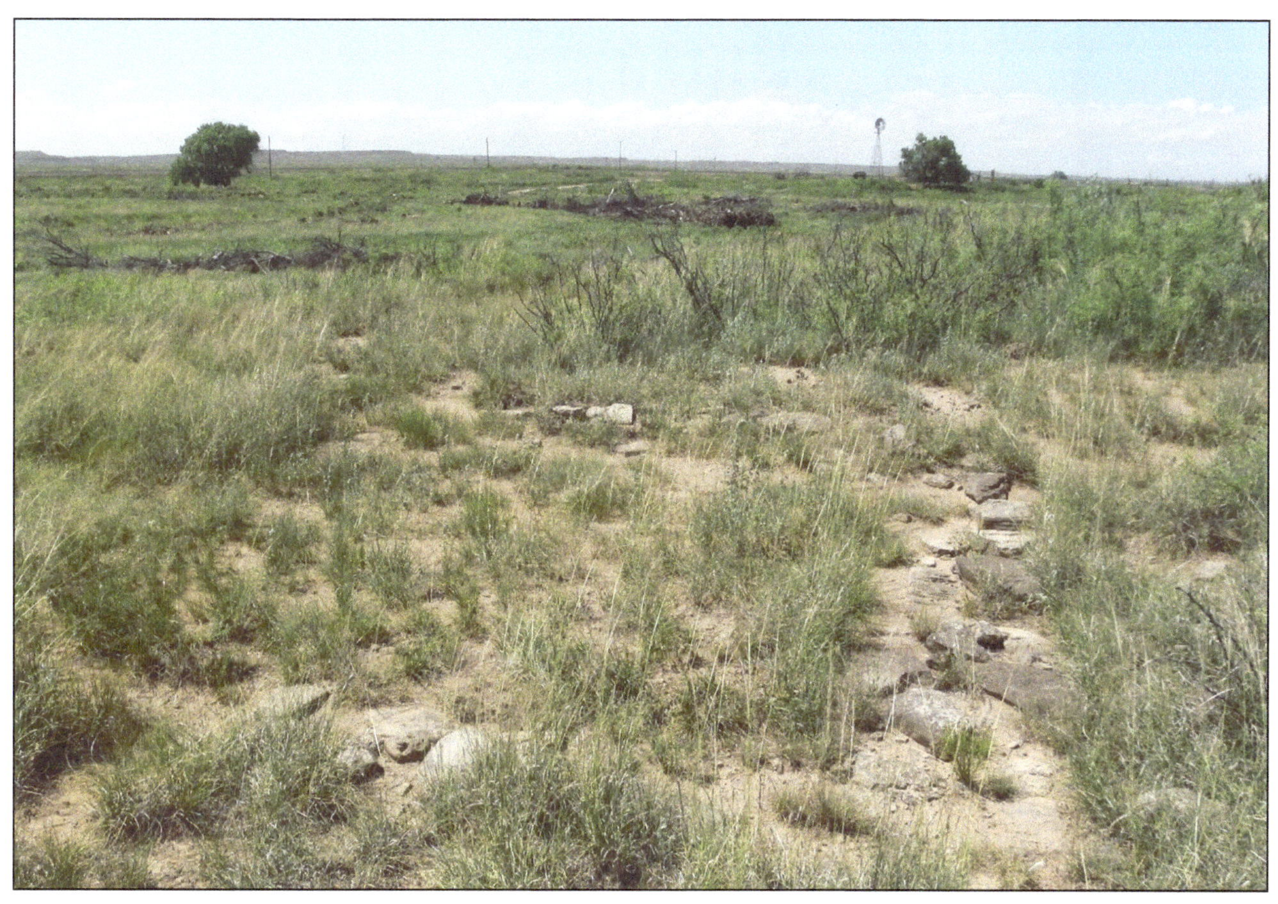

The remains of the stone house in Stinking Springs

Prisoner

The venue for Billy's trial was still set for Doña Ana, but it was a long journey to get there. After being captured in Stinking Springs, Billy and the others were taken back to Fort Sumner, where Billy was allowed to say goodbye to his sweetheart, Paulita Maxwell, while awkwardly being shackled to Dave Rudabaugh. On December 25, the prisoners were taken through Puerto de Luna, where shopkeeper Alexander Grzelachowski hosted what would be Billy's last Christmas dinner. The next stop was Las Vegas, where Billy happily joked and chatted with the people at the train station who wanted to get a glimpse of the infamous outlaw. In a newspaper interview, he told his side of the story and hoped people would realize he wasn't an "animal." It was also at the train station where the posse was confronted by an angry mob, wanting Garrett to release Rudabaugh, who had allegedly killed a jailer there earlier. For his part, Billy was excited about the prospect of a fight but disappointed that he was chained up and would miss the fun. Fortunately, the train left the station before any shooting commenced, and Billy was delivered safely to Santa Fe.

The Kid spent the next few weeks in jail, sending letters to Lew Wallace, reminding him of the pardon he had promised and requesting a meeting with the governor. Wallace ignored his pleas, and at the end of March, Billy was once again en route to his trial. He was taken from Santa Fe through Tularosa, La Luz, and through the Organ Mountains via the San Augustine Pass. On March 29, Billy finally reached the end of the line in Mesilla, and his trial began.

Ira Leonard defended Billy against the murder charge of Buckshot Roberts, saying that since the murder happened in Indian territory, the arrest wasn't valid and was successful in getting the case thrown out. However, after the ruling, Judge Bristol made Leonard step down, and Albert J. Fountain was appointed to defend Billy against the murder of Sheriff Brady. Fountain knew nothing about Billy or his history in Lincoln, but it didn't matter much to Billy's case. Bristol was a friend of Dolan and had been an opponent of McSween. He told the jury that if they thought Billy was even present at the murder of Brady, regardless of whether he was the one who actually killed him, they should consider him responsible. The jury followed Bristol's instructions, and the verdict came back as guilty, making Billy the only participant in the Lincoln County War who was condemned for his crimes. Billy was sentenced to hang on May 13, 1881. Since Billy had no money for an appeal, he was taken back to Lincoln to wait for his execution.

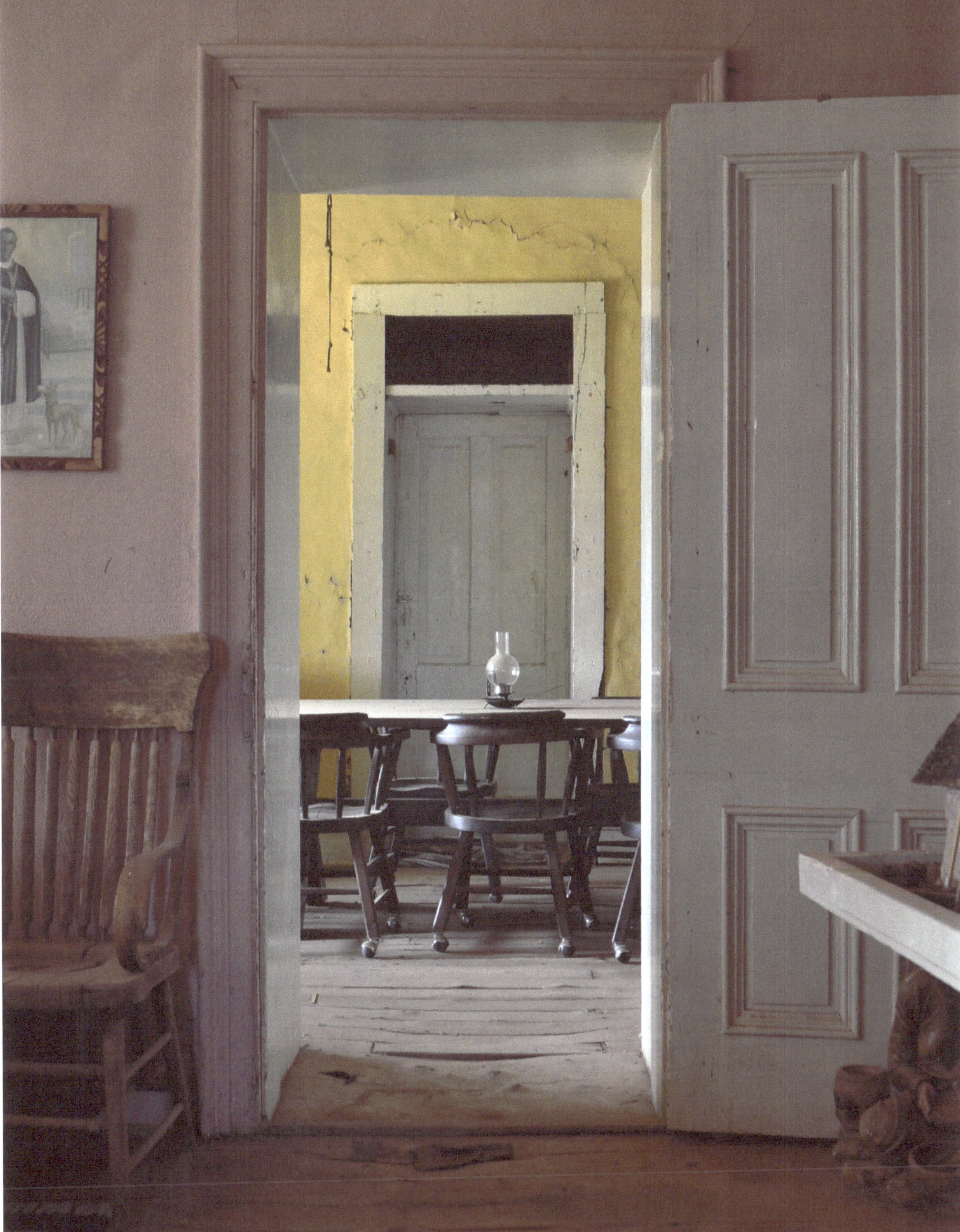

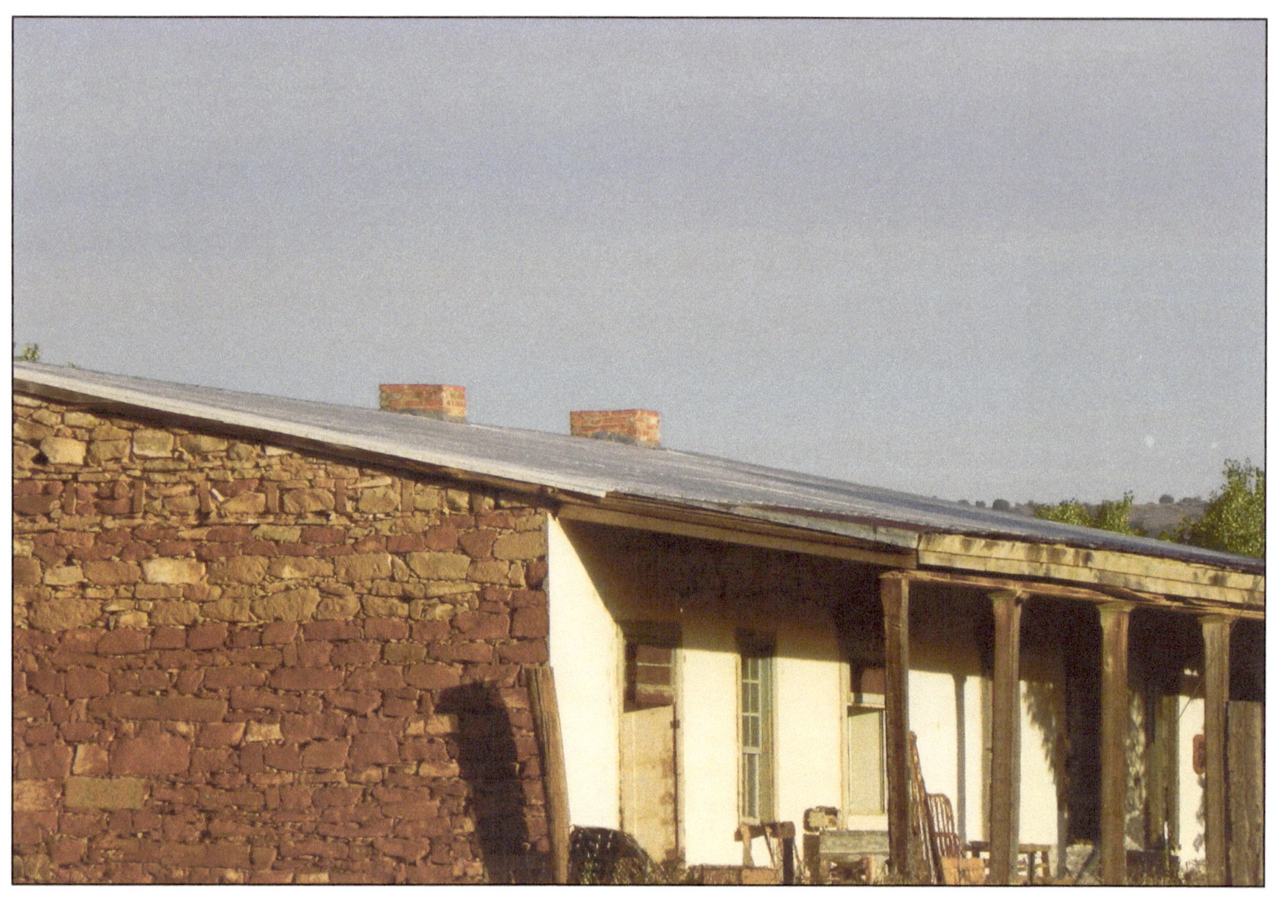

Previous Page: The Grzelachowski house interior where Billy had his final Christmas dinner

Above: The Grzelachowski house exterior

Opposite Page Top: Las Vegas, New Mexico

Opposite Page Bottom: The Las Vegas train station

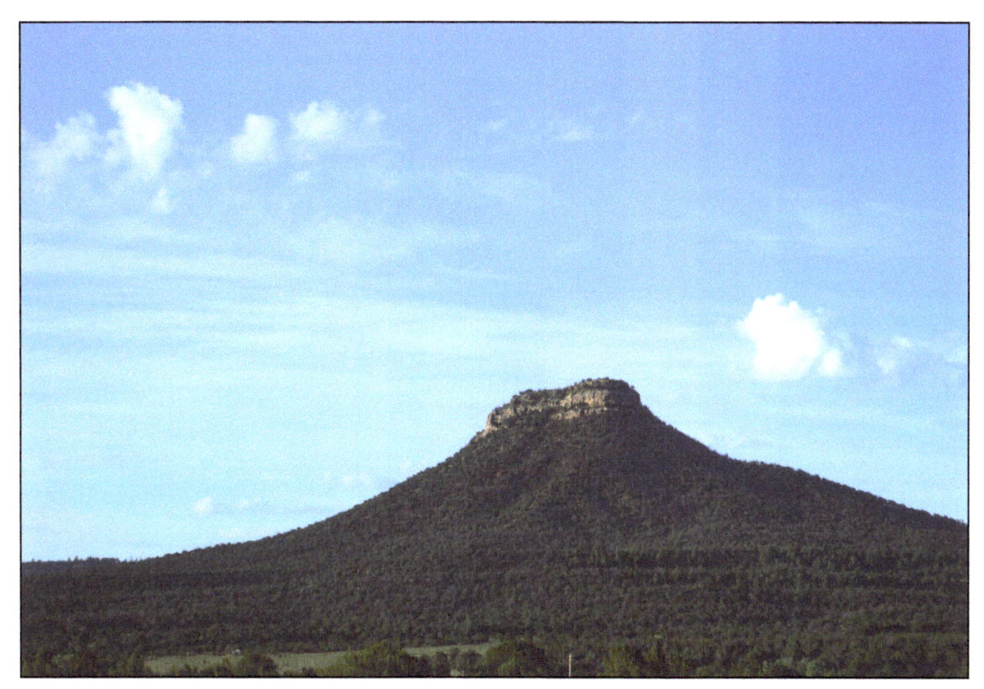

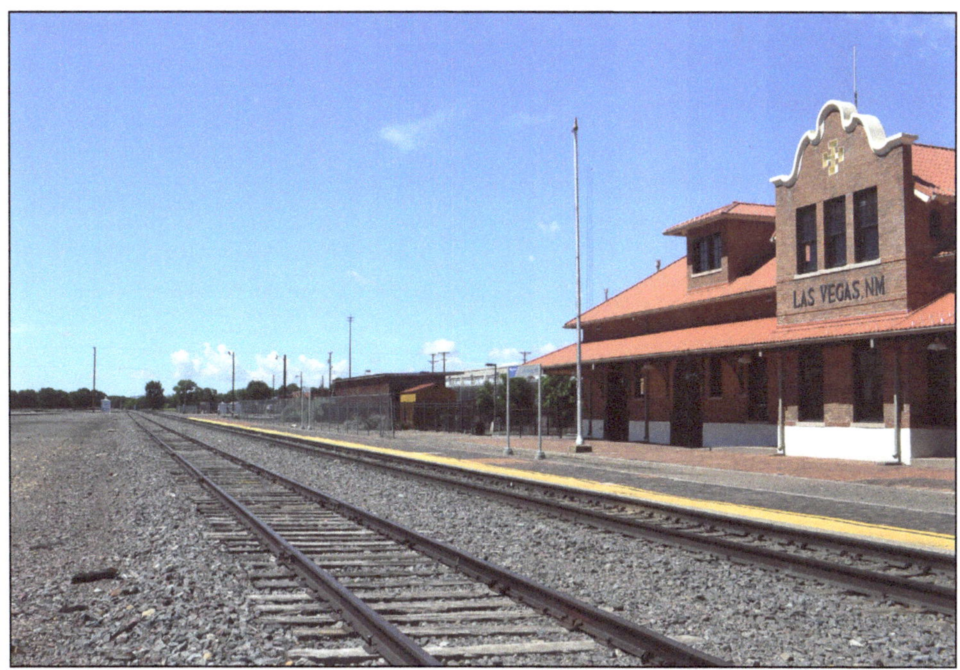
LAS VEGAS, NM

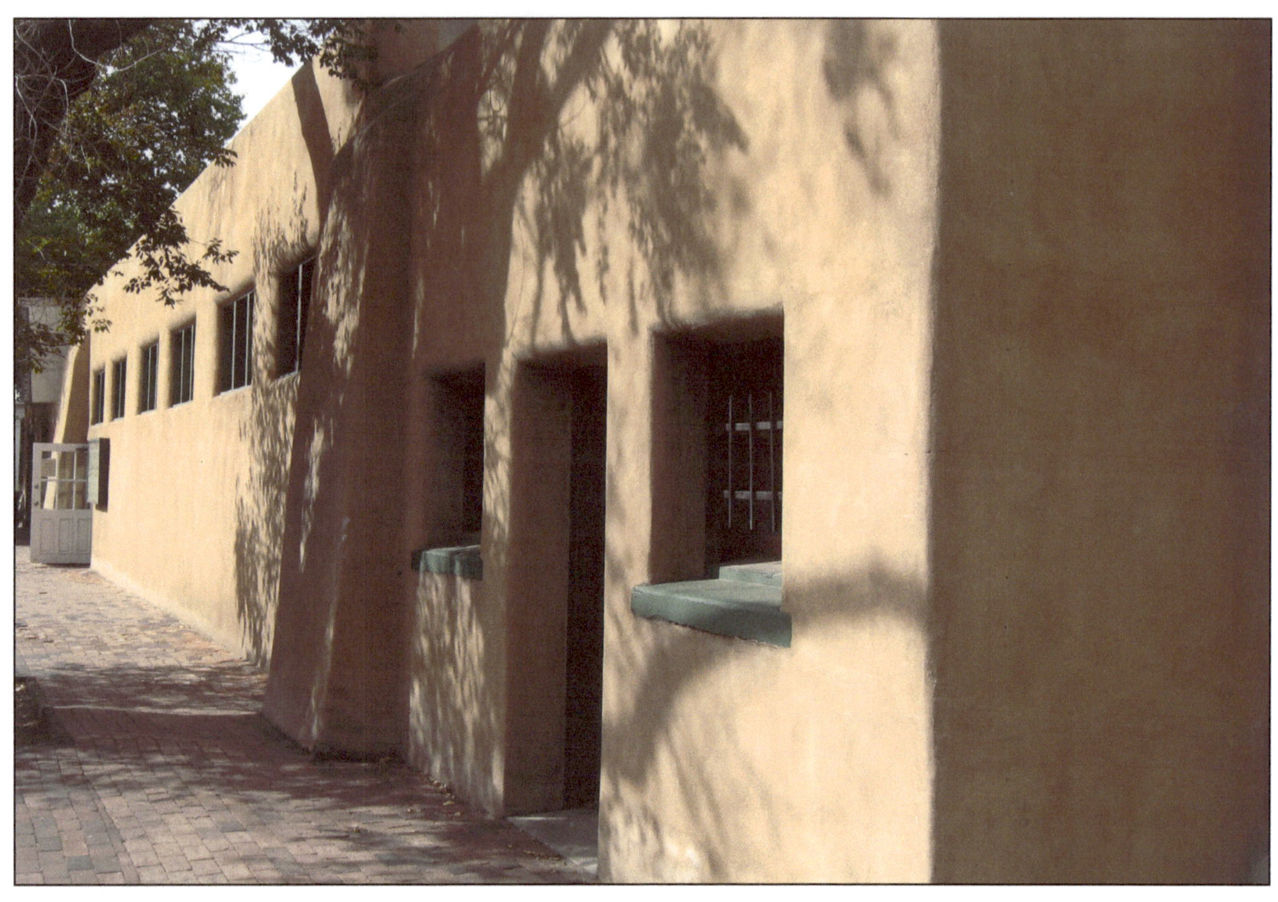

The Palace of the Governors was just blocks from the jail and housed Lew Wallace's office.

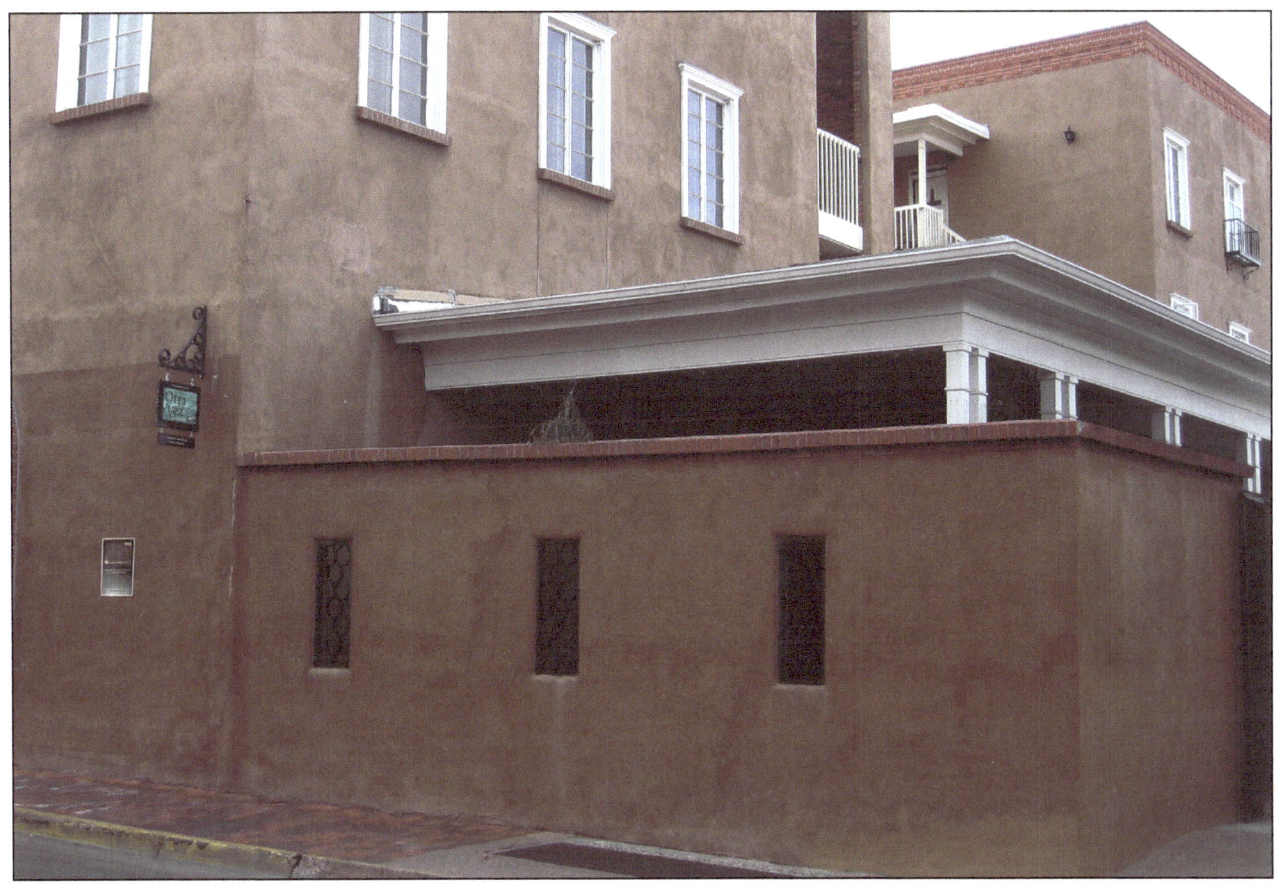

The former Santa Fe jail

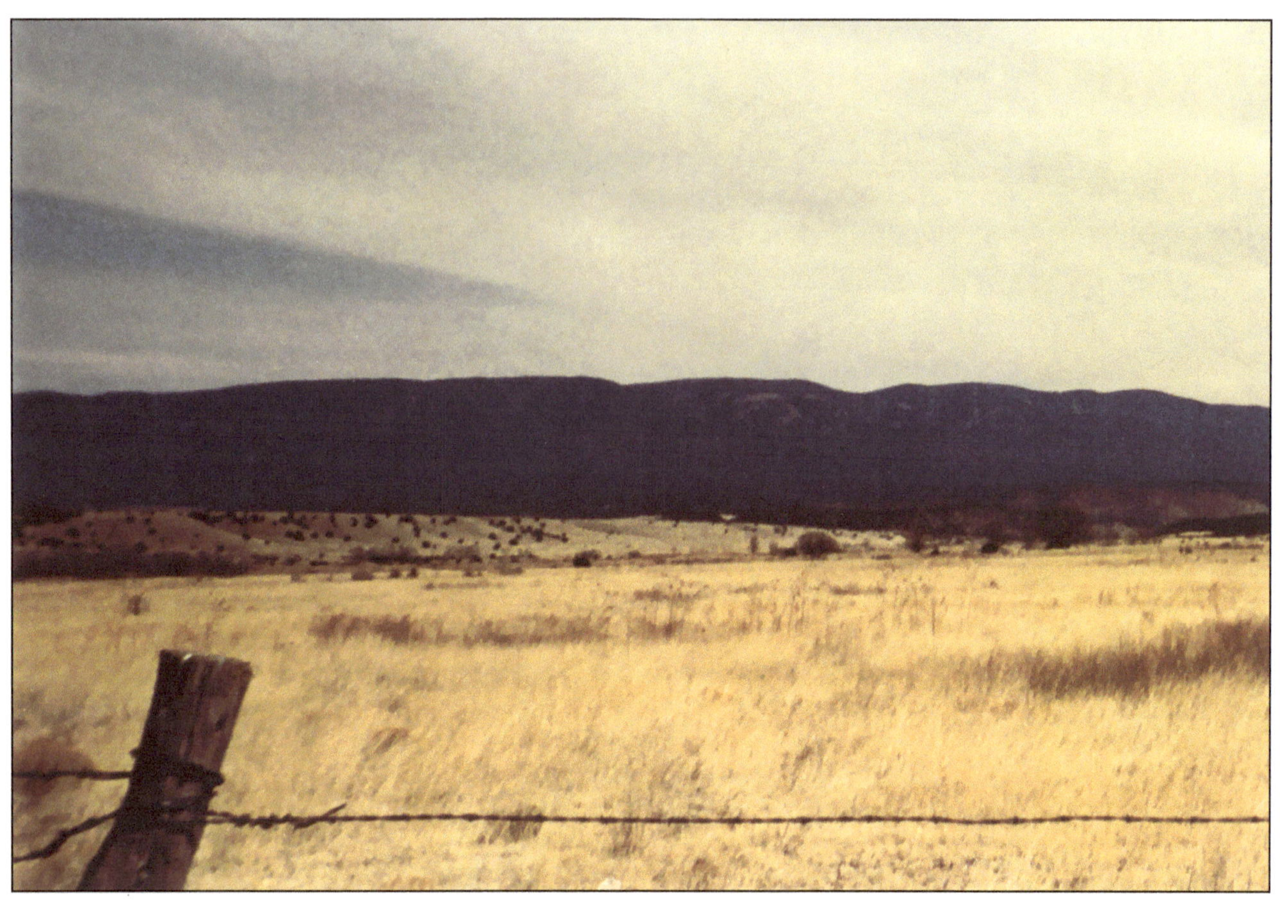

Above: Tularosa

Opposite Page Top: La Luz

Opposite Page Bottom: The Organ Mountains

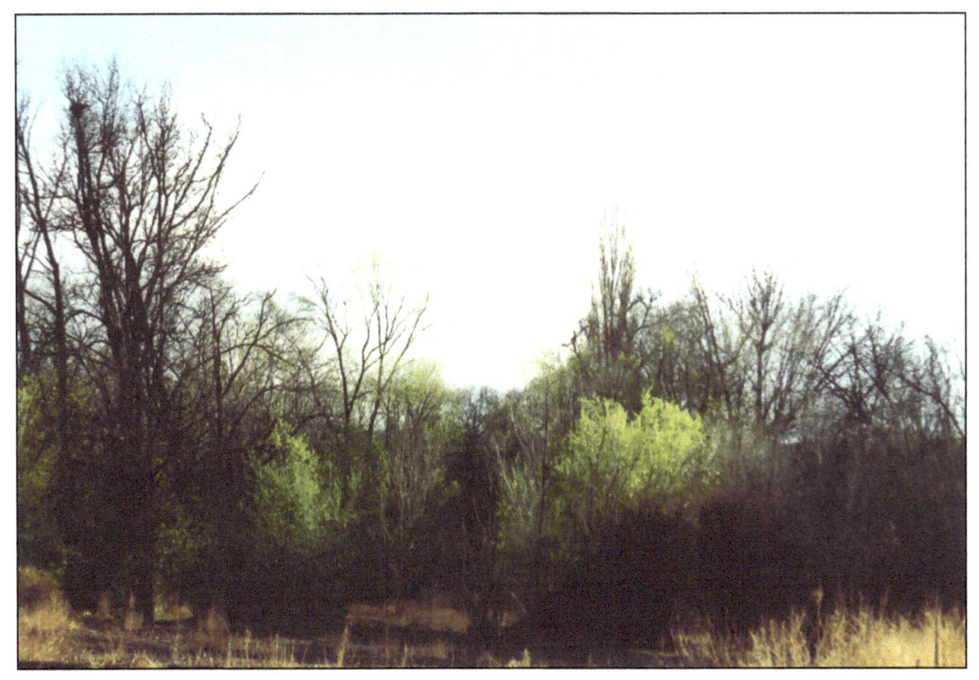

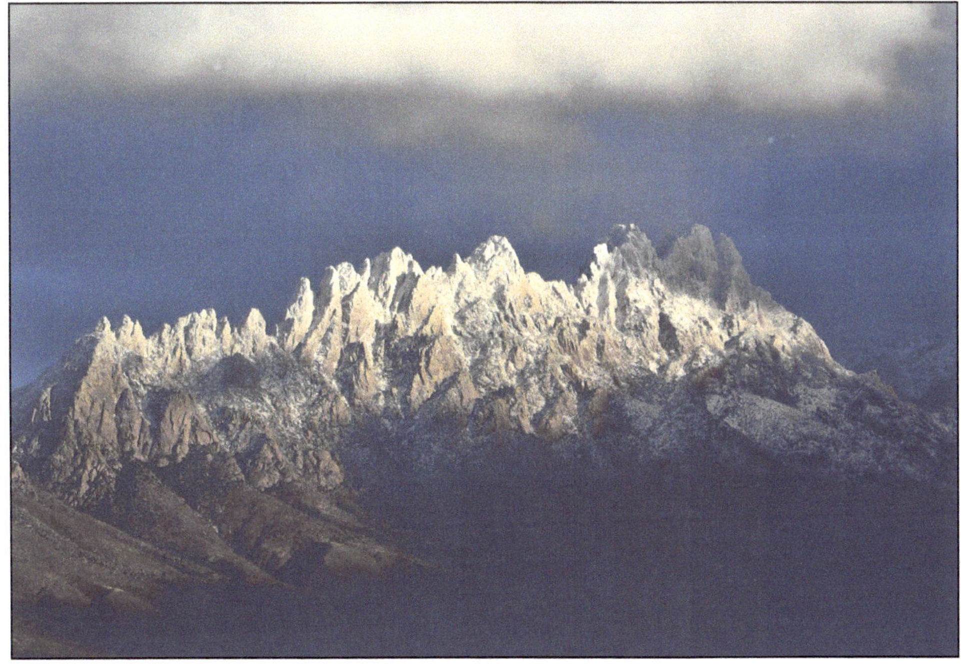

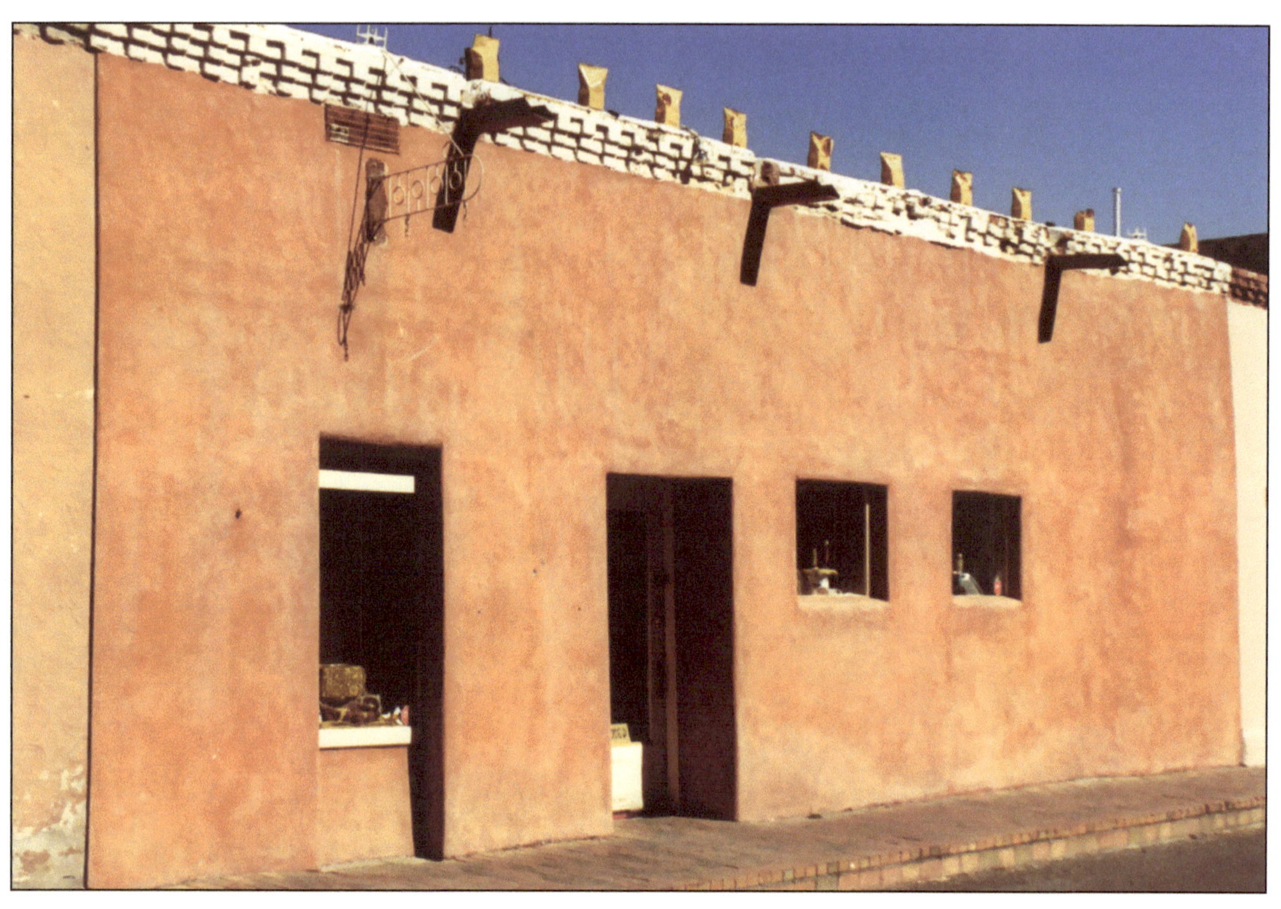

The Mesilla courthouse

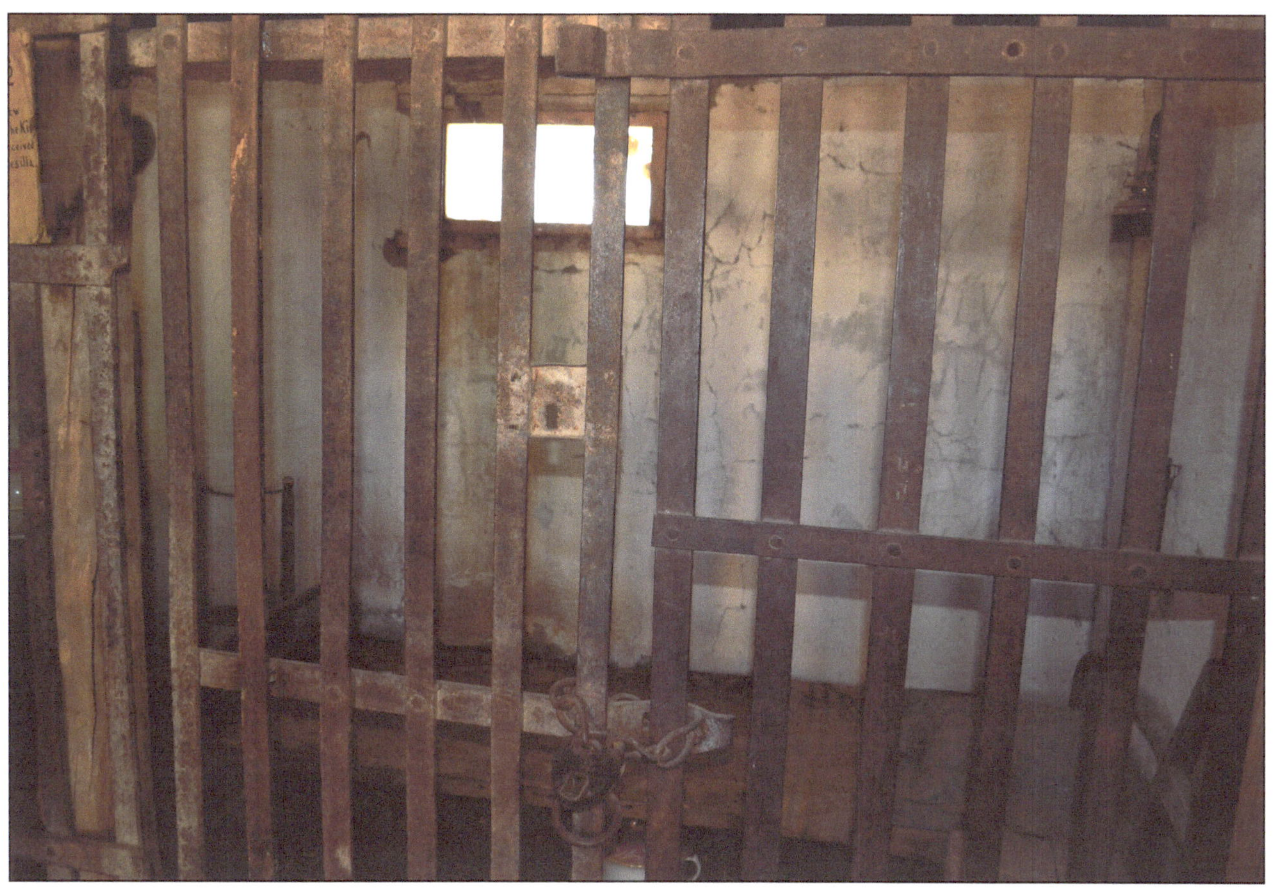

The Mesilla jail was located on the opposite side of a courtyard behind the courthouse. It's long since crumbled, but Billy's jail bars have been preserved in the Gadsden Purchase Museum a few blocks away.

Escape

Once Billy was back in Lincoln, he was taken to the new courthouse—formerly the Murphy-Dolan store—where he was segregated from the other prisoners and held in a room upstairs. Since there were no cells, Billy was shackled at the hands and feet and was guarded around the clock by Garrett or one of his two deputies. J. W. Bell was amicable enough towards Billy and treated him well. However, Billy's other guard, Bob Olinger, hated the Kid, and the Kid hated him. Olinger was on the Murphy-Dolan side during the war and had murdered one of Billy's good friends—shooting him in the back. Olinger never missed an opportunity to taunt Billy by waving a shotgun in his face, daring him to attempt an escape, and counting down the days until the hanging. But that day never came.

Billy had only been in Lincoln for about a week when he had the chance to make one of the most daring escapes in American history. Billy waited patiently until April 28, when Garrett was in White Oaks collecting taxes, and Olinger was across the street at the Wortley feeding the other prisoners. Some versions of events say Billy asked Bell to take him out to the privy, and when they headed back up the stairs, Billy got the drop on Bell—however, no witnesses reported seeing either Billy or Bell leave the building. What *is* known is that Billy got his hands on a gun. He most likely got Bell's by slipping out of his manacles and hitting Bell in the head with them before wrestling his gun away.

Once armed, Billy told Bell not to yell or run and that he wouldn't hurt him. Bell tried to get help anyway, and Billy was forced to shoot. As Bell stumbled down the stairs and out the back door to die, Billy broke into the armory and found Olinger's shotgun. Now even more well-armed, Billy returned to his room and waited at the window for Olinger to run across the street after hearing the gunfire. Once Olinger was underneath him, Billy yelled, "Hello, Bob!" and Olinger looked up. Billy fired and blasted Olinger with buckshot, killing him instantly. Billy then shuffled out onto the balcony and fired the second barrel into Olinger's dead body before breaking the shotgun over the railing and throwing it down, saying Olinger would never threaten him with that shotgun again.

From the balcony, Billy addressed the crowd that had gathered. He told them he had no intention of hurting anyone—he just wanted to leave. No one rode out to notify Garrett.

Billy spent the next hour trying to get out of his leg irons, only managing to break the chain between his feet. It was enough to mount a horse, so he had someone fetch one from the nearby corral, joking that he wished it had been Garrett's. When he tried to mount the horse, it got spooked from the chains and threw Billy off. But Billy just laughed and tried again. Once he was finally astride, he rode out of town, "whistling like a free man."

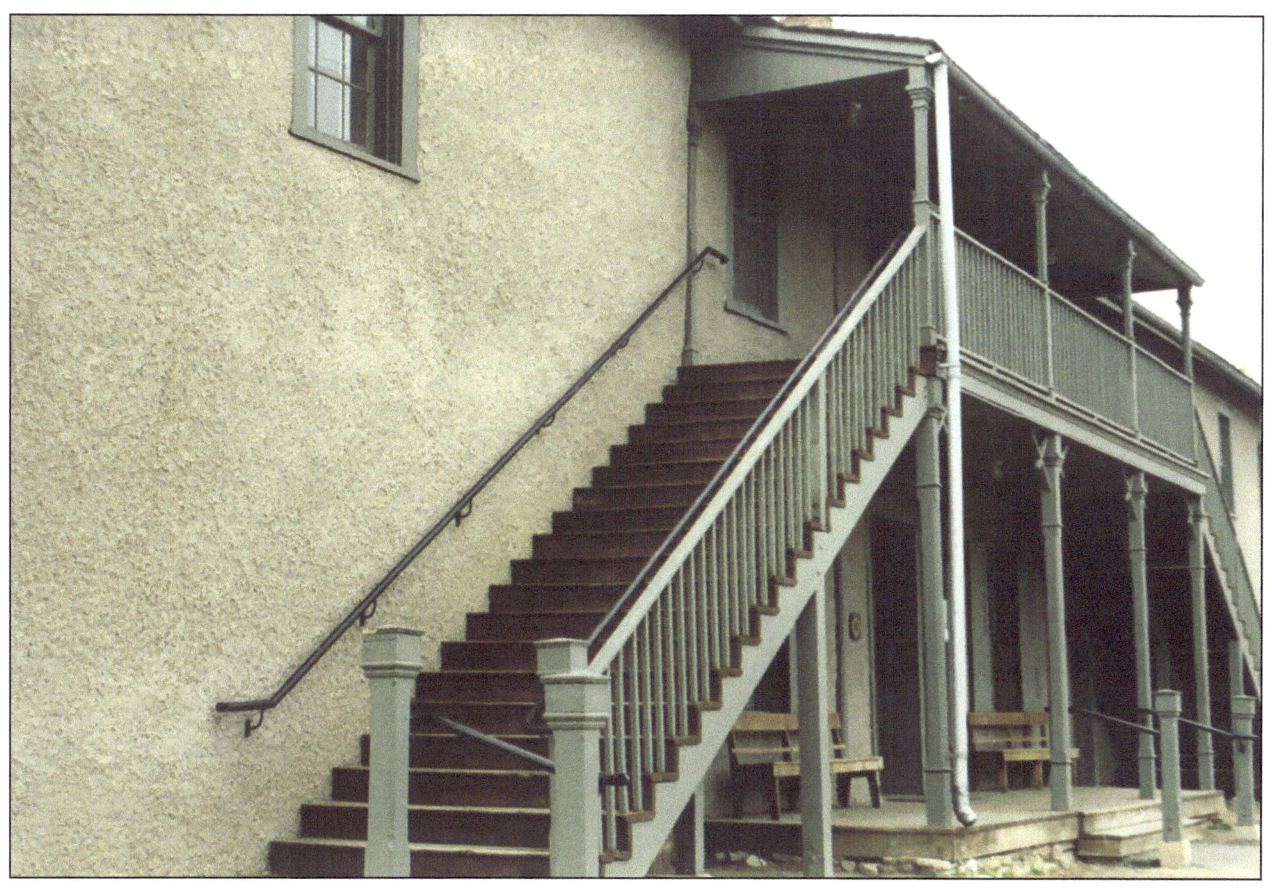

Previously known as "The House," the imposing headquarters of L. G. Murphy & Co. became the courthouse after the end of the Lincoln County War. Prisoners were held in an upper room, but Billy was separated and held across the hall next to Garrett's office.

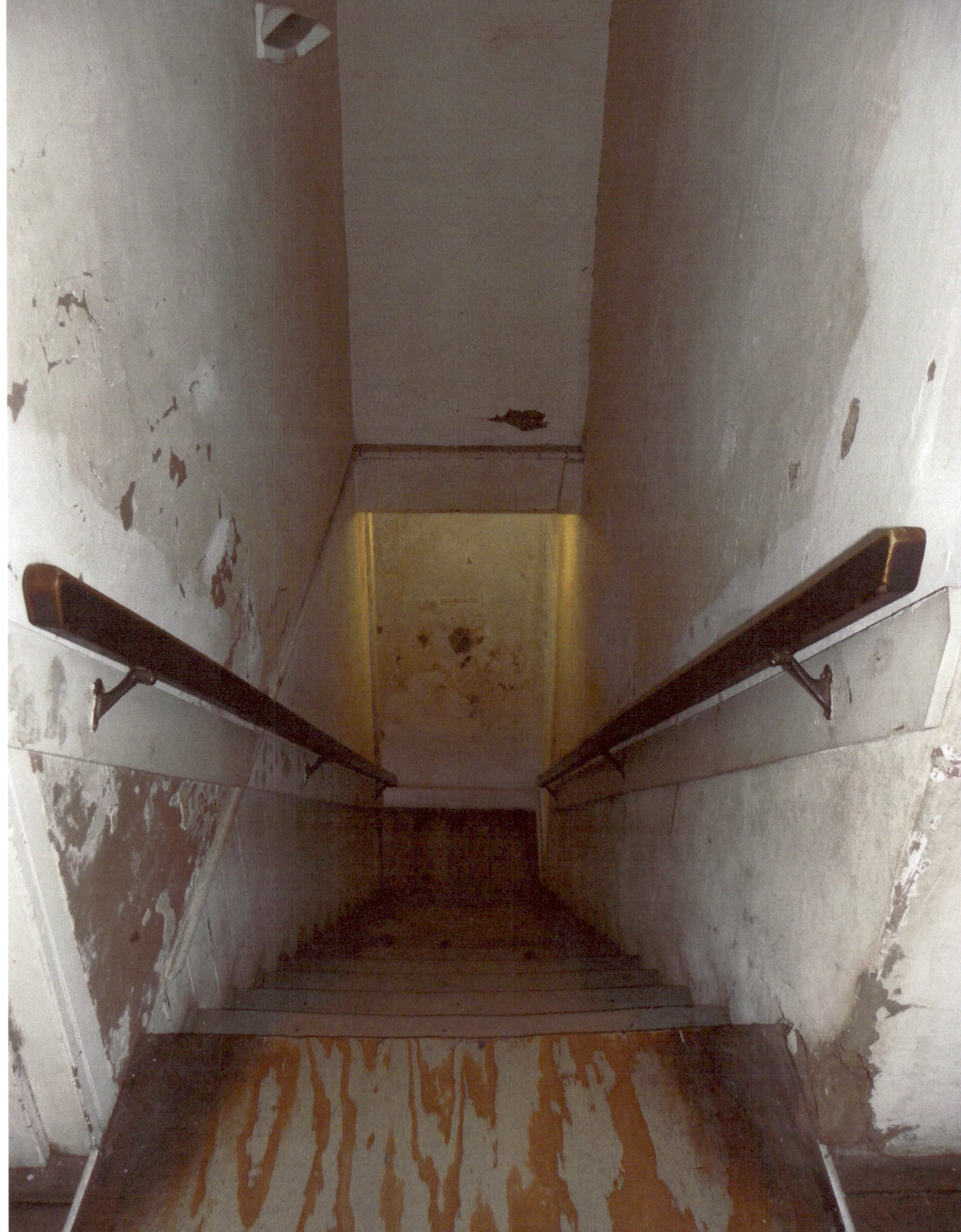

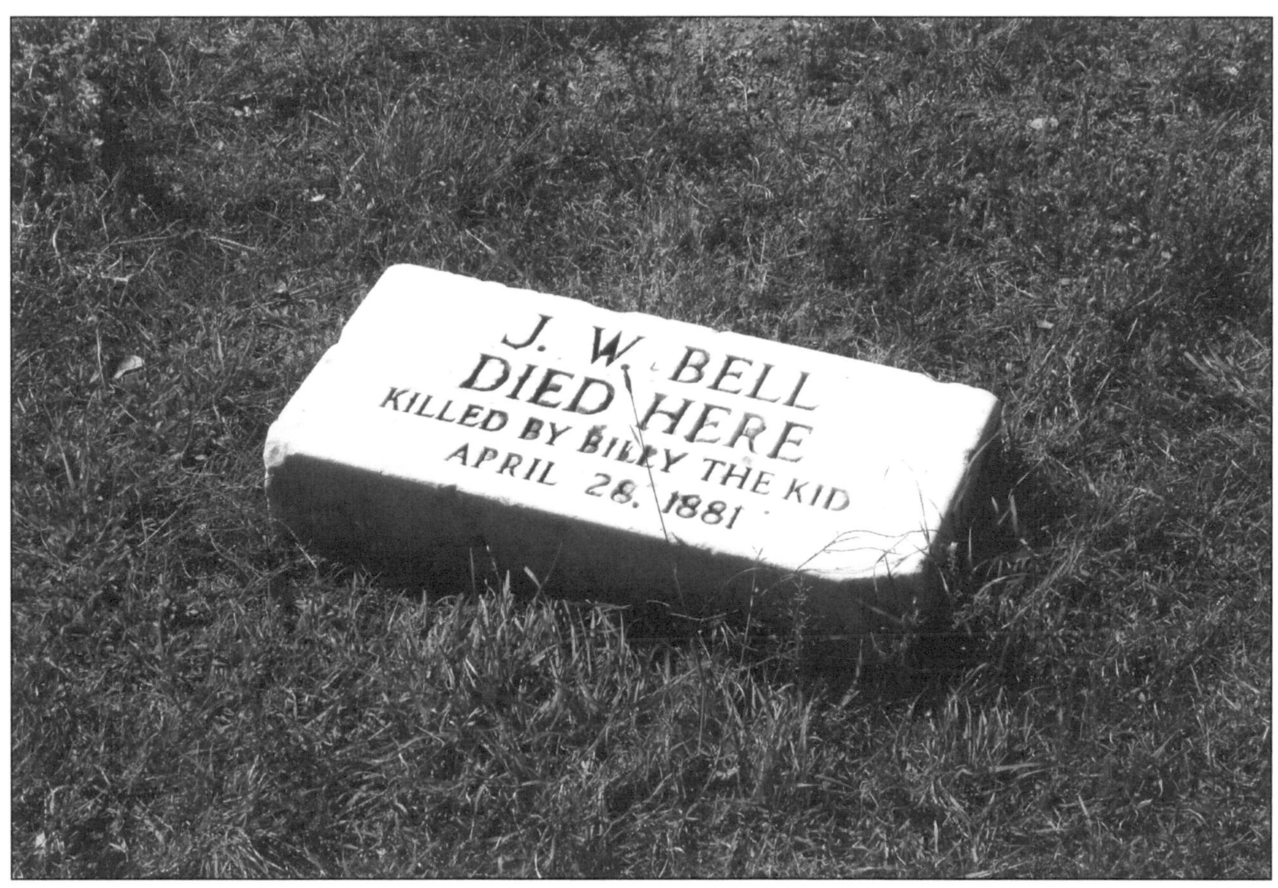

Opposite Page: The staircase where Billy shot Bell

Above: Bell's death marker behind the courthouse

Following Page Left: The armory

Following Page Right: "Billy's Window," from which he shot Olinger

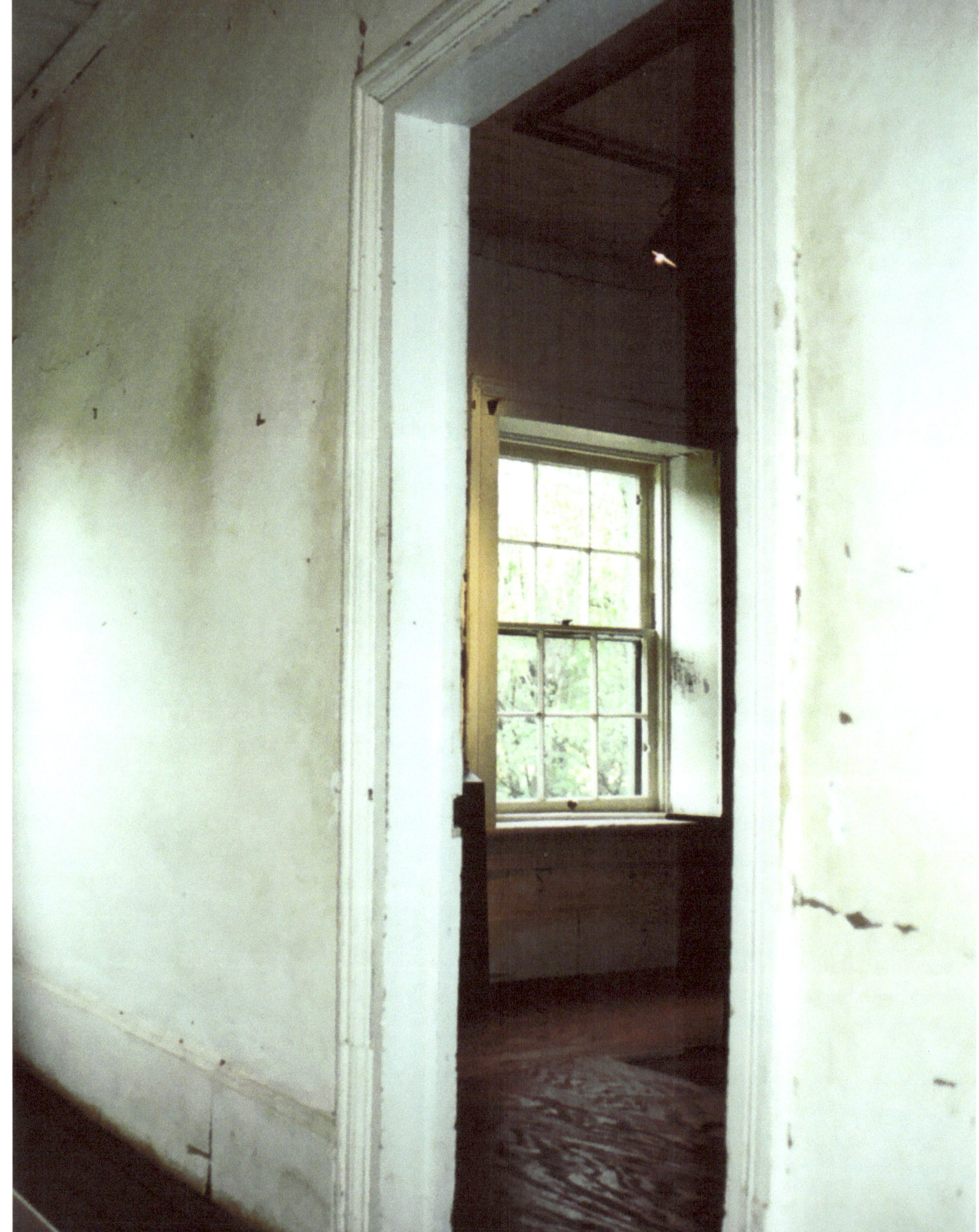

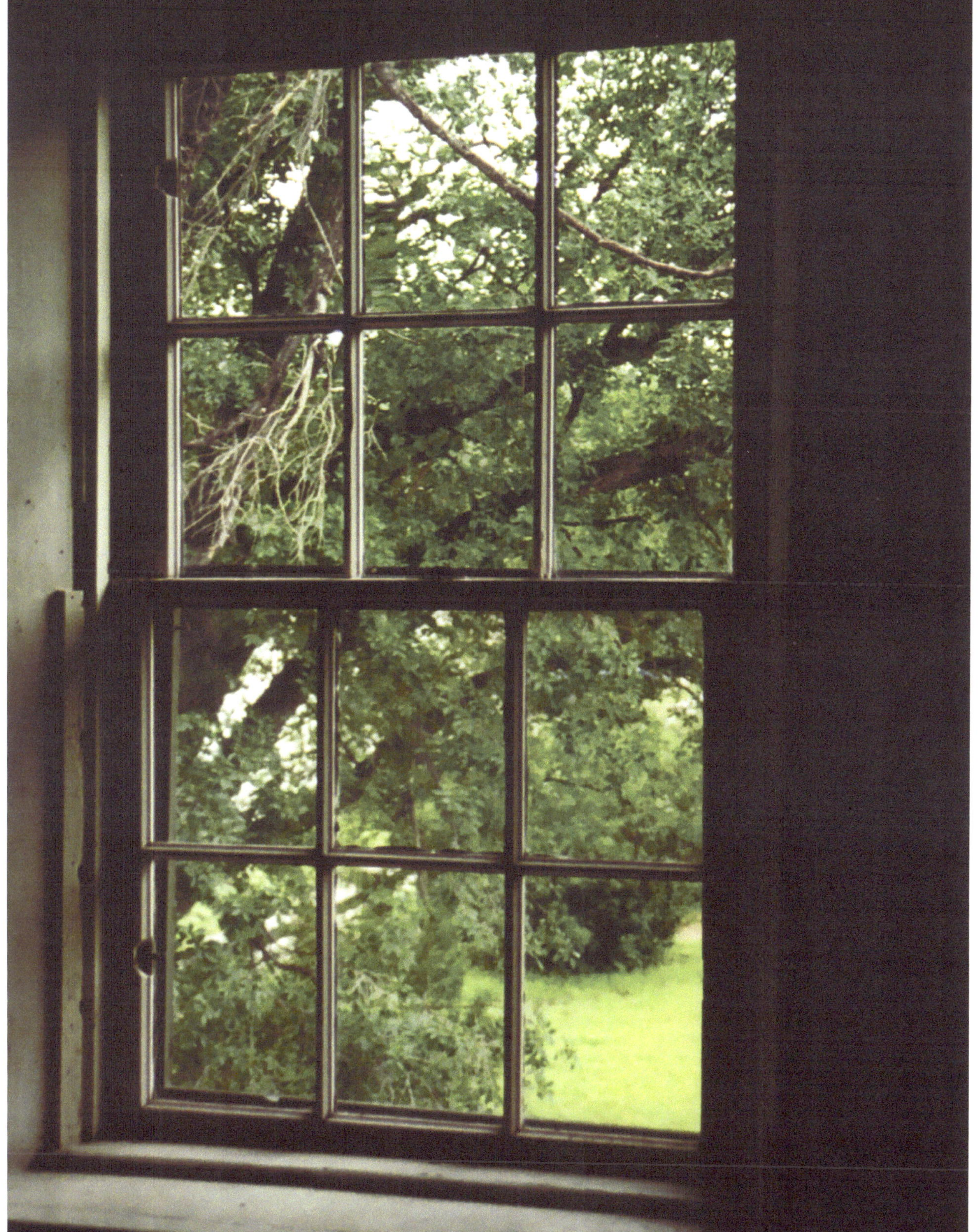

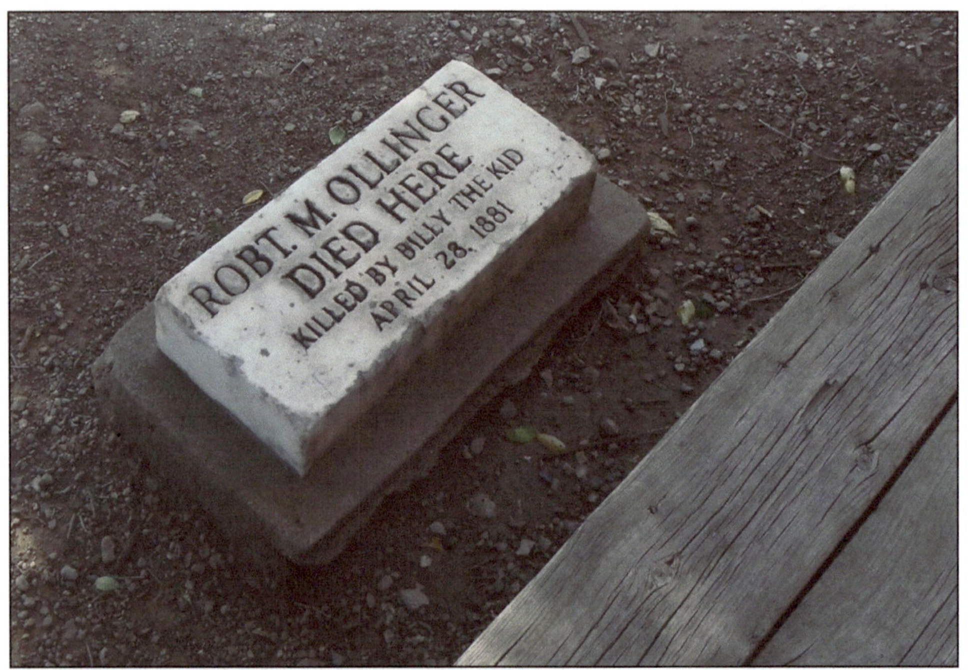

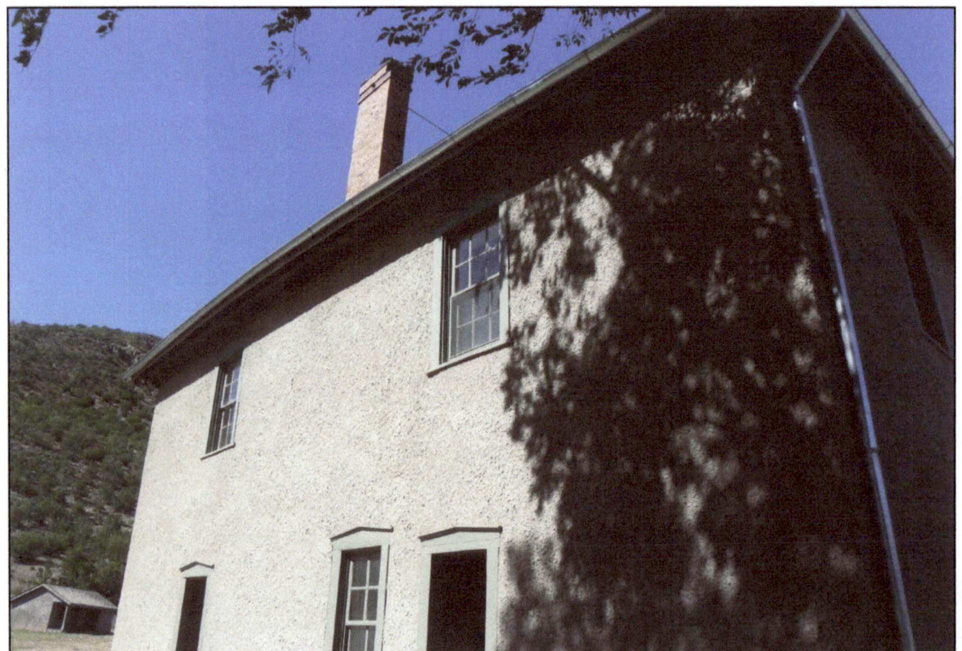

Top: Olinger's death marker beneath Billy's window

Bottom: Billy's window exterior

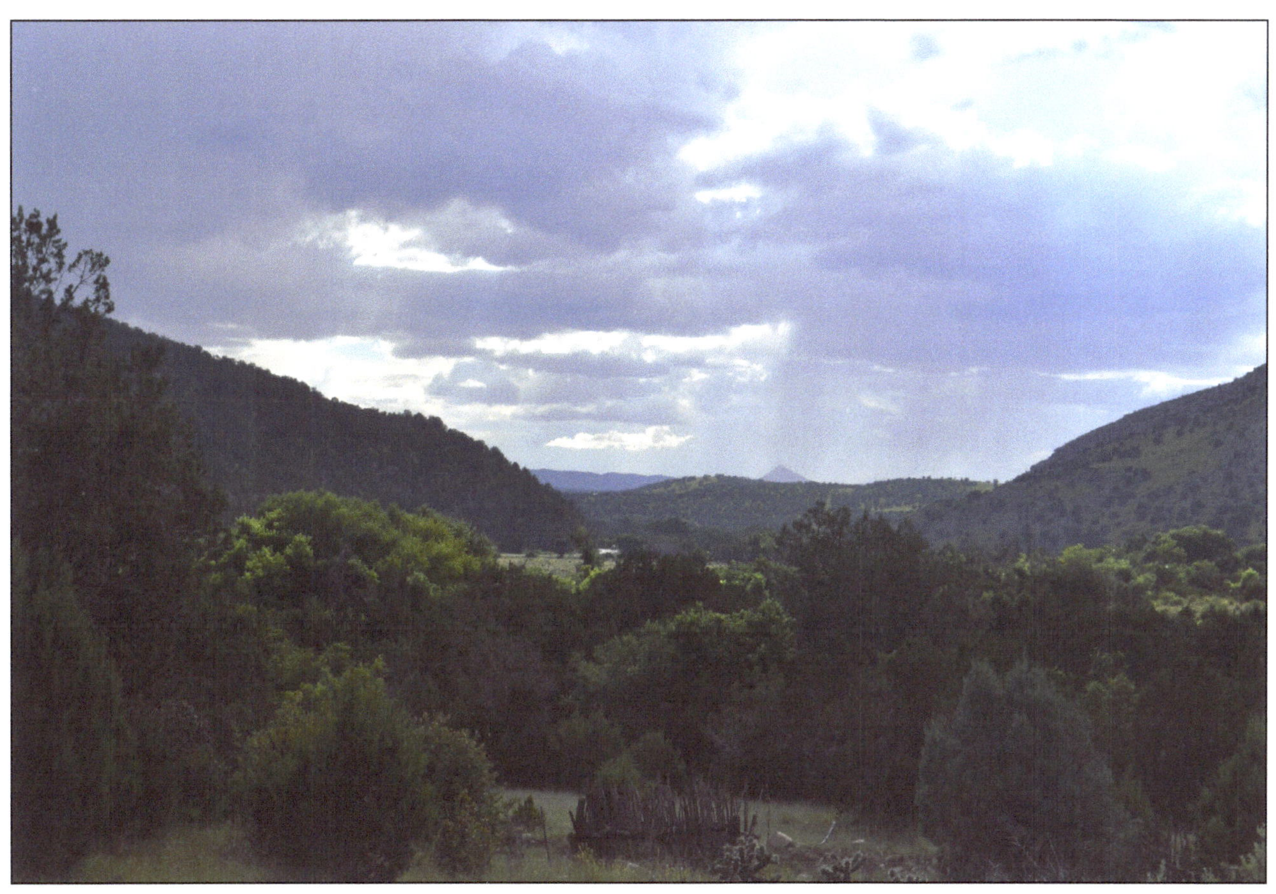

Salazar Canyon. After Billy escaped, he rode to his friend Yginio Salazar's house where Salazar helped him remove his shackles.

Return to Fort Sumner

After his escape, Billy again found refuge in Fort Sumner. It's long been believed that he returned for Paulita Maxwell, hoping to convince her to run off to Mexico with him. Whatever his reason for staying was, Billy spent several weeks hiding in and around Fort Sumner. And even with a price on his head, his friends were loyal; none of them informed Garrett where he was. But Billy also had enemies, and Garrett had spies; he soon figured out where to look for the Kid.

Billy usually remained hidden during the day and ventured into Fort Sumner at night. Around midnight on July 14, 1881, Billy rode into town just after Garrett and his two new deputies, John Poe and Kip McKinney, had arrived. While Billy went to a friend's home to rest, Garrett and his deputies went to the nearby Maxwell house to inquire about Billy's whereabouts. At his friend's home, Billy took off his hat and boots and asked for something to eat. He was told that Pete Maxwell had butchered a heifer that morning, so Billy got a knife and crossed the parade grounds to the Maxwell house to cut off a piece of meat.

Billy passed Garrett's deputies, who, having never seen Billy, mistook the boy in his stocking feet for one of Maxwell's hired hands. But Billy was suspicious of the strangers and asked in Spanish who they were. They told him not to worry about them. Billy didn't like that answer and stepped into Pete Maxwell's darkened bedroom.

Unable to see Garrett sitting on Maxwell's bed, Billy asked in Spanish who the men outside were. Maxwell didn't answer, but Billy suddenly realized they weren't alone. The Kid anxiously asked again, "*¿Quien es? ¿Quien es?*" ("Who is it?"). Rather than answer Billy's question, Maxwell whispered to Garrett, "That's him."

Billy's hesitation was his downfall. Garrett pulled his gun and fired into the darkness, unknowingly hitting Billy just above the heart. Garrett, fearing the Kid's retaliation, fired a second time, hitting a piece of furniture. Maxwell, terrified, ran outside, and Garrett quickly followed. The only sound left in the room was Billy moaning—dying. William Henry McCarty, alias William H. Bonney, alias Billy the Kid, was dead.

Once the men had collected themselves, they lit a candle to make sure that it really was Billy in the room and that he was indeed dead. Deluvina, a servant of the Maxwells' who was particularly fond of the Kid, was among the first to arrive after hearing the gunshots. Upon learning that "her boy" was dead, she started sobbing and swearing at Garrett while hitting him in the chest. Deluvina wasn't the only one upset by the loss. After Billy was carried to the carpenter's shop and laid out on a table, several women in town washed his body, dressed him in one of Pete Maxwell's shirts, and lit candles, sitting vigil with him for the rest of the night.

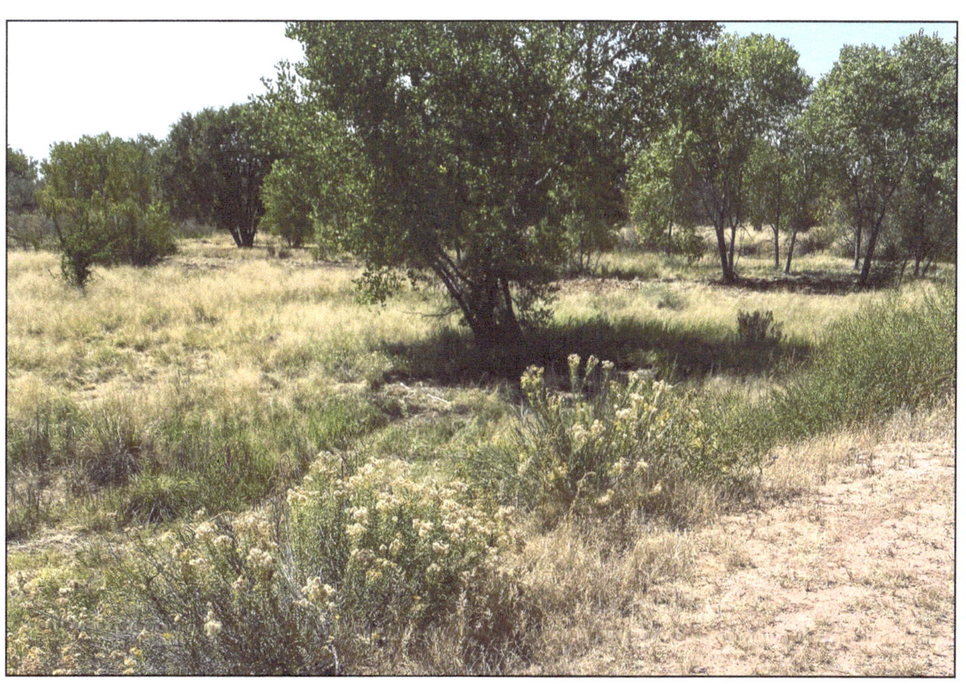

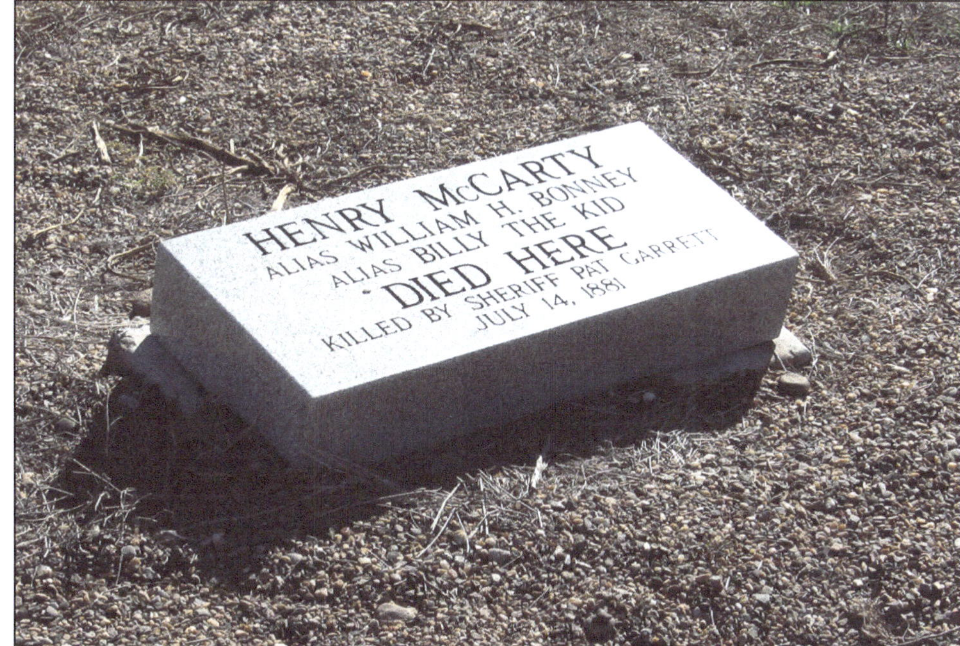

Top: Due to the same flooding of the nearby Pecos River that destroyed the other fort buildings, nothing remains of the Maxwell House where Billy was killed.

Bottom: Billy's death marker

The End

On July 15, Billy was laid to rest in the Fort Sumner cemetery near his friends, Tom Folliard and Charlie Bowdre. Nearly everyone in town followed the wagon carrying the coffin to the cemetery. No priest was available to conduct the service, but a man referred to as the "Sanctified Texan" read a passage from scripture: Job 14:1-2, "Man that is born of a woman is of few days and full of trouble. He cometh forth like a flower, and is cut down: he fleeth also as a shadow, and continueth not." He finished by saying, "Billy cannot come back to us, but we can go to him and will see him again up yonder, Amen."

Opposite Page: Pals. Tom Folliard, Charlie Bowdre, and William H. Bonney, alias Billy the Kid

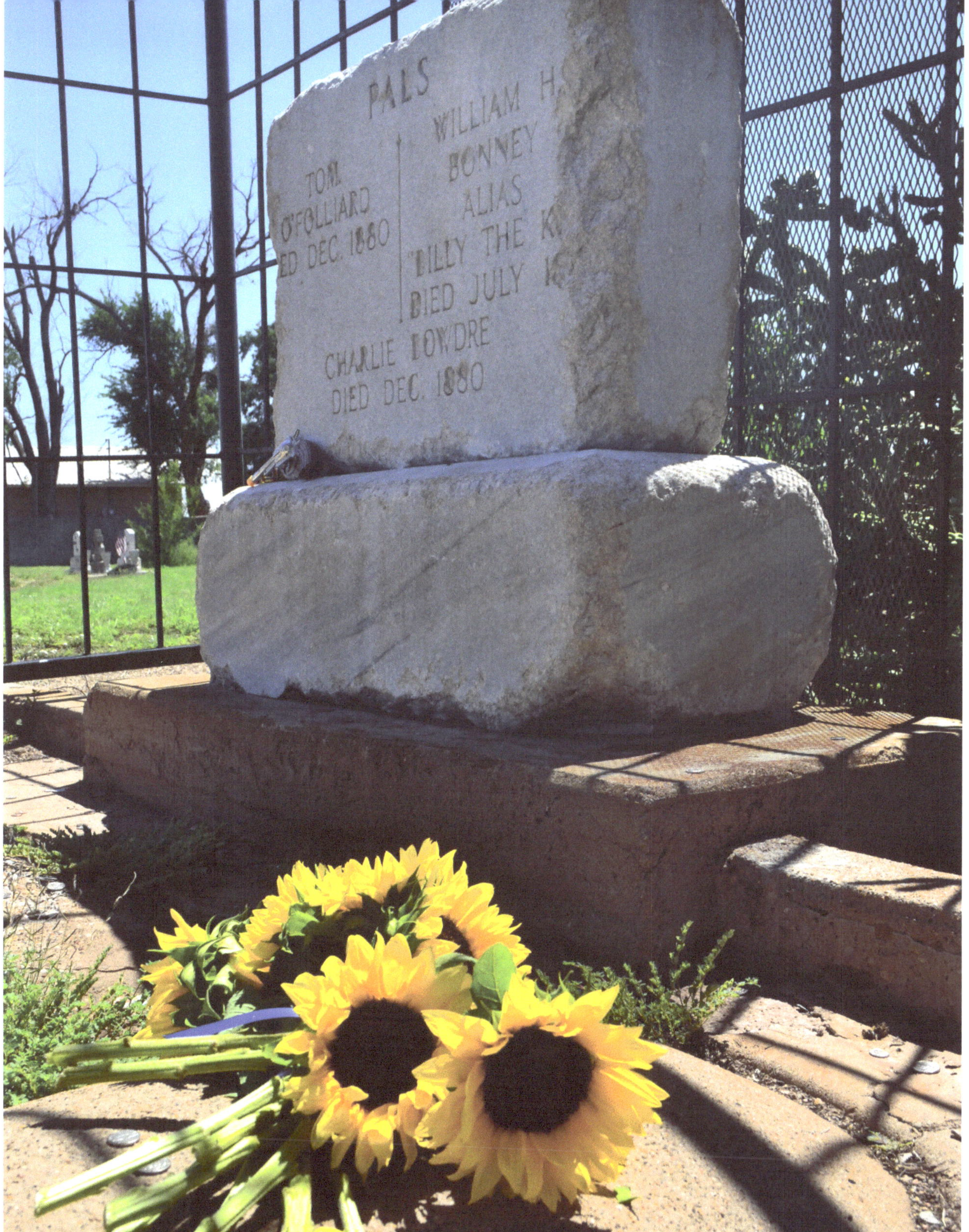
PALS
TOM
O'FOLLIARD
ED DEC. 1880
WILLIAM H.
BONNEY
ALIAS
"BILLY THE K
DIED JULY 1
CHARLIE BOWDRE
DIED DEC. 1880

Afterword

After his untimely death, Billy's legend continued to spread, and he grew to be one of the most infamous outlaws in history. Over 140 years later, the stories of his life still attract people—people like me. I spent years in search of the famed outlaw. What I found was a boy who loved adventure and who was fiercely loyal to the people around him. Had his life not been cut short, had he not been pursued relentlessly across the territory, and if Lew Wallace had granted the pardon he promised, Billy could have become a respectable citizen. But they were determined to take his life. Billy wanted the fighting to end more than anyone, but the greed and corruption in the territory kept him on the run. He was braver and more honest than the men in power at the time, and I believe it is for this reason that Billy the Kid became a hero in New Mexico's history.

Opposite Page: Billy's Grave, Fort Sumner, July 14, 2012

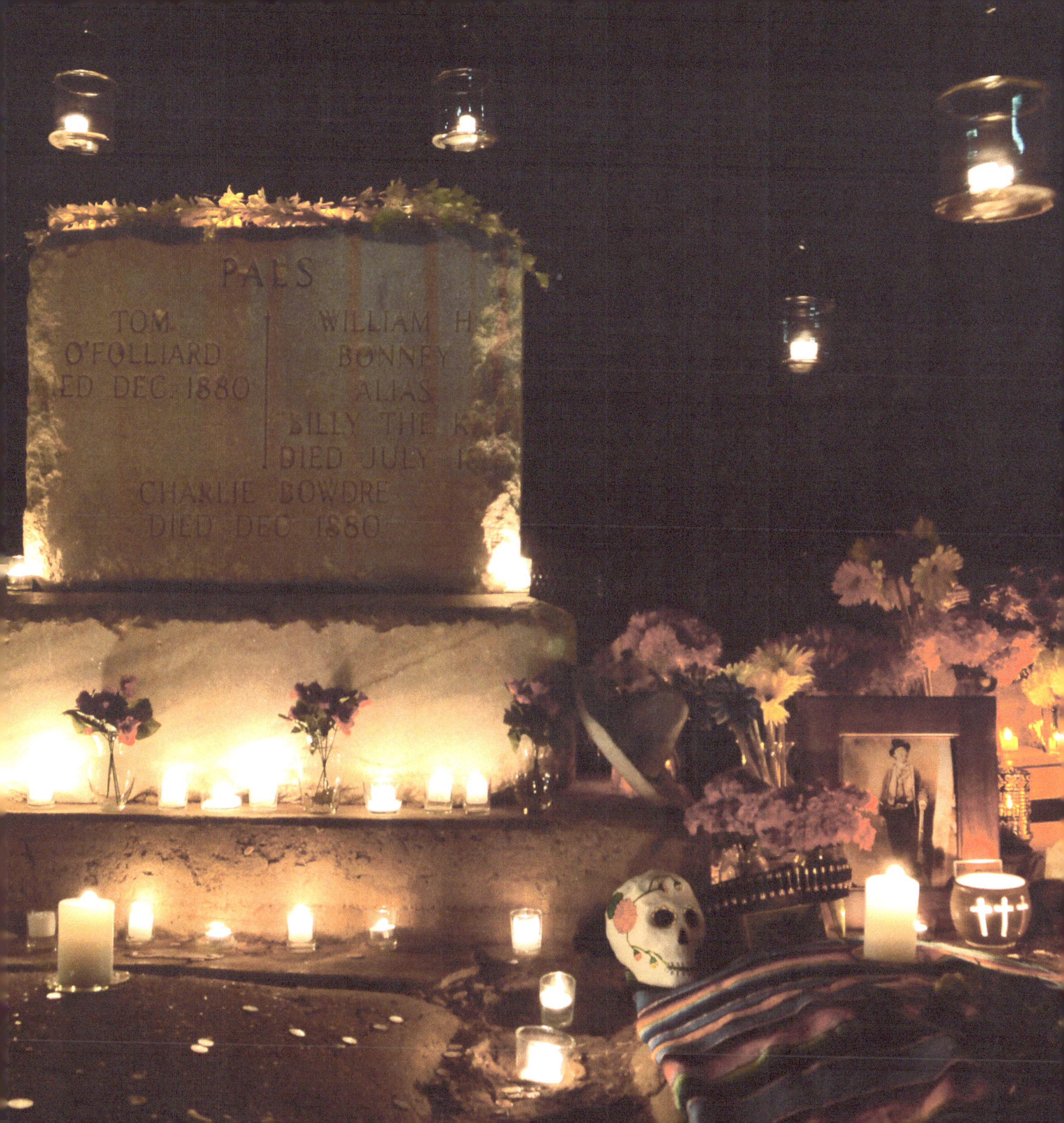
PALS
TOM
O'FOLLIARD
ED DEC. 1880
WILLIAM H
BONNEY
ALIAS
BILLY THE K
DIED JULY 1
CHARLIE BOWDRE
DIED DEC 1880

Bibliography

Banks, Ann. *First Person America.* New York: Alfred A. Knopf, Inc., 1980.

Bell, Bob Boze. *Bad Men: Outlaws & Gunfighters of the Wild West.* Phoenix: Tri Star, 1999.

Bell, Bob Boze. *The Illustrated Life and Times of Billy the Kid.* Phoenix: Tri Star, 1996.

Burns, Walter Noble. *The Saga of Billy the Kid.* New York: Konecky & Konecky, 1953.

Eastwood, Johnny. "Portales Springs." *Outlaw Gazette* Volume XXIV [2011]: 7

Nolan, Frederick. *The Billy the Kid Reader.* University of Oklahoma Press, 2007

Nolan, Frederick. *The Lincoln County War: A Documentary History.* Santa Fe: Sunstone Press, 2009.

Nolan, Frederick. *The West of Billy the Kid.* Norman: University of Oklahoma Press, 1998.

Otero, Miguel Antonio Jr. *The Real Billy the Kid.* Houston: Arte P˙blico Press, 1998.

Priestley, Lee. *Billy the Kid: The Good Side of a Bad Man.* Las Cruces: Yucca Tree Press, 1993.

Thomas, David G. "'Dirty' Dave Rudabaugh." *Outlaw Gazette* Volume XXXIII [2023]: 5

Thomas, David G. *The Trial of Billy the Kid.* Las Cruces: Doc 45 Publishing, 2021.

Tuska, Jon. *Billy the Kid: His Life and Legend.* Albuquerque: University of New Mexico Press, 1994.

http://fpcsantafe.org/who-we-are/history

http://www.shakespeareghostown.com/outlaw.html

Acknowledgements

A big thanks to Linda Pardo, Shelly Buffalo Calf, Steven and Sarah Kretschmer, Chris and Robyn Jones, Billy Roberts, Tim Roberts, John LeMay, Tamsin Silver, Elizabeth Fackler-Sinkovitz, Lucas Speer, and Tara Pipes for being present for much of the journey, whether we were searching out the sites or talking about the Kid for endless hours. And thanks to Bob Boze Bell, Drew Gomber, Fred Nolan, and Bob McCubbin for always being generous with your time and answering any random Billy questions I had. Also, to the Billy the Kid Outlaw Gang for keeping his memory alive. To Dr. Baker, Mr. Hout, and Ian Morrison for setting me on this path. And finally, thanks to my dad for giving me my first camera and to my mom for indulging my obsession.

About the Author

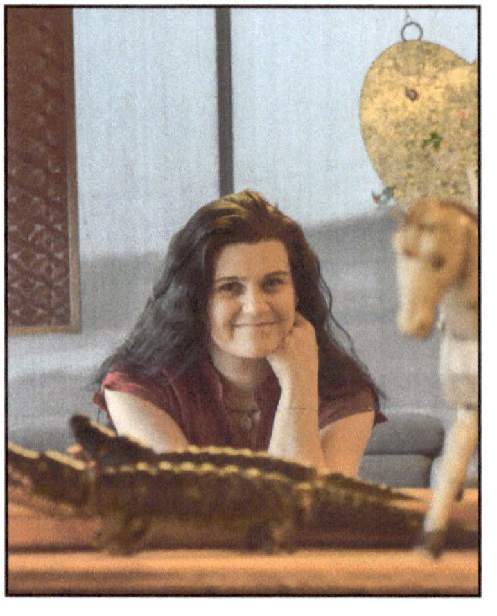

Lori Ann Goodloe was born and raised in Las Cruces, New Mexico. At age fifteen, she became enamored with Linda McCartney's photography and studied photography, art, and design at Grand Canyon University in Phoenix, Arizona. In 2000, she graduated with a Bachelor of Arts. It was that same year she started writing this book as a photography assignment, and her teacher suggested that she try to get it published. The first edition was published in 2009. In the years following, she continued her research and travel and added dozens of new photos and more detailed history. In 2012, Lori was elected president of the Billy the Kid Outlaw Gang, and in 2011, she became editor and designer of their *Outlaw Gazette.*

www.ingramcontent.com/pod-product-compliance
Lightning Source LLC
LaVergne TN
LVHW070507120826
845147LV00031BA/256

* 9 7 9 8 9 9 1 3 1 8 8 9 1 *